GW00818910

Gardens in my Year

Gardens in my Year

Inside Australian Gardens

Holly Kerr Forsyth

NH
NEW
HOLLAND

First published in Australia in 2000 by
New Holland Publishers (Australia) Pty Ltd
Sydney • Auckland • London • Cape Town

14 Aquatic Drive Frenchs Forest NSW 2086 Australia
218 Lake Road Northcote Auckland New Zealand
24 Nutford Place London W1H 6DQ United Kingdom
80 McKenzie Street Cape Town 8001 South Africa

Copyright © 2000 in text: Holly Kerr Forsyth
Copyright © 2000 in photographs: Holly Kerr Forsyth
Copyright © 2000 New Holland Publishers (Australia) Pty Ltd

All rights reserved. No part of this publication may be reproduced, stored
in a retrieval system or transmitted, in any form or by any means,
electronic, mechanical, photocopying, recording or otherwise, without the
prior written permission of the publishers and copyright holders.

National Library of Australia Cataloguing-in-Publication Data:

Forsyth, Holly Kerr, 1953–.
Gardens in my year: inside Australian gardens

Includes index.
ISBN 1 86436 628 1

1. Gardens—Australia. 2. Gardening—Australia. 3. Australian
newspapers—Sections, columns, etc. I. Title. II. Title: Inside Australian
gardens. III. Title: Weekend Australian.

635.0994

Publishing General Manager: Jane Hazell
Publisher: Averill Chase
Senior Editor: Monica Ban
Copy Editor: Jan Hutchinson
Designer: Kerry Klinner
Reproduction: Colourscan (Singapore)
Printer: Tien Wah Press

Cover: *Clematis* 'Red Corona'.
Back cover: Busker's End.
Title: 'Green on green', says Dean Havelberg of his garden, Hillview.
Page 6: Summer exuberance! The delightful *Schoenia cassineana*.

Contents

Preface

This book has come about because the readers of my weekly column in *The Weekend Australian Review* would often ask for information contained in one of the 111 stories that I'd written by the end of the millennium. It's not always possible to respond to all requests for photocopies or 'back issues'. A permanent home for the columns, which are the stories of the people I have met and the gardens that I love, seemed the solution. Hence, *Gardens in My Year—Inside Australian Gardens.*

Garden writers and photographers are enormously privileged, in many ways. They daily indulge their passion for gardens; their hobby is their work. Most importantly they share garden tales with people who often become friends. They hear stories of rare treasures sought, swap information on obscure plant dealers and hunters; they receive gifts of treasured plants and more than occasionally a meal and a roof over their head.

It's not all beer and skittles, or more appropriately, coffee and cake. And there are times when it's downright dangerous. People often say to me: 'what a nice life you lead, wandering around gardens, chatting to nice people'. I like to assure them, of course, that there are many mornings when I'm up before the birds, to be at a garden to catch the soft dawn light. Then there are the times when you're lost and lonely, and homesick for hearth and home.

There are times when 'country time' takes on a new meaning; when an owner has told you it will take 'just a couple of hours' to find his place from whatever garden you've been photographing. Five hours later, tired and cross, you arrive—but not before you've become lost and stopped at a house to ask the way. Pushing past old stone walls, calling out for the owner, you tread on something that feels like a piece of irrigation pipe. You look down, just in passing. It's a snake, luckily with its head already into the dry stone wall! You finally arrive at your destination and tell the owner about the drama of finding him, describing for him your black snake. 'Oh!' he says heartily, 'that was a tiger snake'. Years later you are still telling the tale.

Then there was the time a neighbour, down in the Southern Highlands of New South Wales, gave me permission to crawl under his fence to photograph his stable, which, once every year, is covered in those glorious roses, 'Wedding Day' and 'Albertine'. A truly amazing sight if you can catch it at its peak. So over the lawns at our weekender I went, trundling behind me some 40 kilograms of camera gear. Now what he hadn't told me was that the grass in his paddock, across which I had to wheel my gear to reach the stable, was waist high and that the paddock was full of cows and all that accompanies them. Nor did he warn me that his electric fence was on, so that when my tripod caught it, the electric reaction was immediate. Heart pounding, I got the shot.

My companion on those early morning forays is my little radio, along with a cup of tea. Staying with friends in country Queensland a couple of years ago, I would be up early to set up camera and tripod and wait for the rising light. I'd creep around the kitchen in the half dawn, fill the kettle, make my tea, return to the camera and wait. I remember thinking that the tea tasted somewhat strange. One morning I noticed my friend filling the kettle from a certain brass tap. 'Why do you use that tap?' I enquired. 'All the other taps in the house are fed from the lagoon', she replied. I then knew why my early morning cups of tea had been tasting brackish.

Electric fences, snakes, country roads and booked-out hotels aside, I thank all the garden owners who have shared their gardens with me, and allowed me to photograph; who have given advice, offered beds and most welcome cups of tea—and many wonderful meals and glasses of wine—and some great company.

My thanks to *The Australian* newspaper for allowing me, every week, to indulge my passion for talking about gardens. My grateful thanks to Shelley Gare who championed the idea of a weekly garden column in *Review*, a section in Saturday's *Australian* that was born in September 1997. Shelley gave me the most marvellous vehicle by which to talk about the plants, the gardens and the gardeners I love. I have had terrific editors at the *Australian*, among them Jim Jenkins, Helen Anderson, Scott Coomber and Eliot Taylor with whom I've shared much talk and laughter about all manner of things, other than gardens. My thanks to News Limited for believing that we need to enrich and replenish our souls with good food, wine, books, film—and with gardens—even though we may also be fascinated with politics, finance and more serious world issues.

And my thanks to the readers, who make it all worthwhile.

Holly Kerr Forsyth

Summer

Aberfoyle

Barbara Lightbody inherited her garden, Aberfoyle, situated near Mount Gambier in South Australia, from her mother-in-law in 1965 and wasted no time in pushing out the fences. Her husband Max acquiesced, under sufferance, she says. The result, some 35 years later, gives great joy to both the owners and the visitors they welcome.

The original garden, created by Max Lightbody's mother on a soldier settlement block was, according to Barbara, 'a colourful, tidy country garden, with hedges, fences, a vegetable garden and a well-kept orchard'. Today you are greeted by a noisy gaggle of guineafowl, Indian runner, Peking ducks and stately geese, which bring up the rear as they waddle, with proprietorial purpose, across the perfect lawns.

The long drive into the garden winds through paddocks in which the Angus cross cattle that are bred on the property graze. On either side of the entrance to the garden is a sturdy pergola covered in the flamboyant rose 'Albertine'; her long, elegant, deep pink buds open to a shell-pink bloom, compensation for the fact that she only performs once each year. Underneath a mass of roses, including the cream, cluster-flowered 'Medeo', the delicate ivory-coloured 'French Lace', 'Seduction' and the tea rose 'Savoy Hotel' flower profusely throughout summer.

The garden, which is more than a hectare in size, is predominantly a rose garden. 'I'd rather cut a rosebush back than daisies,' Barbara admits. Her first love would probably be the hybrid teas, which flower for much of the year. '"Sylvia" keeps going till the end of July and then "Seduction" is not long after.'

The garden is a peaceful balance between massive lawns and generous, curving beds filled with roses. One bed is devoted to 'Sylvia', a very fragrant hybrid tea, pink with coral overtones, and with very red stems. 'It's wonderful for picking,' says Barbara. '"Diamond Jubilee" is just gorgeous, a huge, creamy apricot flower, but balls if it's wet.' Then there's a bed of the magnificent 'Red Devil' with enormous, perfectly shaped, scented flowers and deep green foliage.

Overlooking a large pond is the old shearing shed, built in Mount Gambier limestone which was cut in blocks at the quarry, and which, in December, is covered in the species rose *Rosa gentiliana* looking like a million fragile, pale moths in full flight. The scented flowers have the bonus of orange, oval shaped hips in autumn.

In 1997, the fence separating the old orchard from the garden was moved to create room for more roses. The deep beds here are punctuated with tripods of 'Pierre de Ronsard' showing off its coconut ice colours from spring until Easter. In this part of the garden, Barbara's favourite area, special roses include the hybrid teas 'Temptation', the remontant 'Blue Moon', 'Sweet Sonata' and the mauve-to-pink 'Paradise'.

Barbara struggles to name her favourite rose, but when pushed nominates 'Sylvia' for picking and 'Sweet Sonata' (also known as 'Johann Strauss') for its glorious pale salmon colour, its generous flowering and its willingness to appear in early spring.

Opposite: 'Albertine', a 'once-only' rose, embraces a walkway at Aberfoyle.

Bottom left: *Rosa* 'Duet'.

Bottom right: The apple-green leaves of the Oriental poppy.

How this garden works

* Aged manure from the silage heap mulches the garden beds. Iron chelates are used to counteract iron deficiency in the soil.

* Guineafowl roam the garden controlling beetles and earwigs; Cayuga and Khaki Campbell ducks take care of slugs and snails.

Gingers

The loud chorus of cicadas keeps you company each afternoon and the air is filled with the Christmas scent of massed gardenias and freshly mown grass. Mmm—holidays are coming, and you flashback to your childhood. It only takes one summer garden of *regale* and *auratum* lilies spilling over clipped green hedges, a few flowers of frangipani scattered on the lawn, to make you realise that you can have a marvellous garden in a temperate or sub-tropical climate, if only you would stop pining over the visions of a different paradise in English books.

Landscapers opine about architectural plants, which, to some of us, may mean downright ugly, or even dangerous with those hard leaves—lethal to playing children's eyes. You could describe the gingers as architectural—but perhaps you'd be doing them a disservice, for they are exotic rather than rigid. They are also wonderful garden plants, great for massing; they are fascinating, diverse and deliciously scented.

The Sunshine Coast of Queensland, with its rich volcanic soils, high rainfall and humidity, enjoys perfect growing conditions for ginger. The beautiful sub-tropical and tropical gardens at Yandina's Ginger Factory—which occupy 2 hectares within the 12-hectare factory site—are largely devoted to the cultivation of the many different species of ginger.

There are, in fact, nearly 2000 genera and species within the ginger family (Zingiberaceae), including the edible ginger (*Zingiber officinale*).

These useful landscaping plants can be difficult to locate in nurseries, but here a large range of the species and cultivated varieties—some very rare—is available for sale. There is *Zingiber spectabile*, the stunning golden beehive ginger and a wide selection of *Hedychium*, the most scented genus in the family. Here you will find the very fragrant white ginger lily, *Hedychium coronarium*, which is used for making perfume.

The related *Heliconia rostrata*, which goes by the somewhat exotic common name of 'Hanging Parrot's Beak' and the rare *Heliconia angusta* 'Red Christmas' with its dazzling, red winter flowers, as well as the rare 'Yellow Christmas' and 'Orange Christmas' are also used in the gardens and are on sale in the nursery. There is also the very rare pink torch ginger, the stunning *Etlingera elatior*, from Indonesia, for sale.

Alan Maxwell is Horticultural Director at the Ginger Factory. 'Despite the common belief that gingers are tender tropical plants there are numerous species that are hardy in the colder climates of the Southern states,' he says. '*Hedychium gardnerianum*, which is native to the Himalayas, is probably one of the most cold tolerant. It is also brightly coloured, with a glorious scent. Another cold tolerant genus is the alpinias, with shell ginger (*Alpinia zerumbet*) doing well in Sydney. They are extremely easy to grow, and largely disease free.'

Bottom left: The stunning *Heliconia bihai*

How these gardens work

* Alan Maxwell advises, 'Gingers like well drained, rich soil and regular watering from spring, through summer and autumn. Don't water in winter. Gingers that flower terminally must have the spent stems cut down to ground level as they only flower once per stem'.

* At The Price of Peace, Sandy Freudenstein advises that peonies don't like a lot of water, hate being watered in the sun, and hate to be moved.

* Sandy sprinkles a handful of sulphur around each rosebush to prevent black spot.

The Price of Peace

Sandy Freudenstein and Russell Price have created their glorious garden, The Price of Peace, on a hill close to the south-western New South Wales town of Young. Just 12 years old, the garden combines many different elements and reflects the diverse gardening interests and talents of its owners.

A key theme of the garden is provided by a collection of archways, hand-made by a local blacksmith, which divide the 1 hectare garden into several very different areas. Seven arches, each covered in roses, dissect the first garden walk. There are the mother and daughter roses, 'Zephirine Drouhin' and 'Kathleen Harrop', both thornless and scented. There are arches of 'Lorraine Lee' and the deep red 'Black Boy', bred by Victorian grower, Alister Clark. There are arches covered in 'Dorothy Perkins', 'Cecile Brunner', the clear red 'Altissimo', the vigorous 'Wedding Day' and the repeat-flowering 'Golden Showers'.

Another great love is the bearded iris, and there are 42 different varieties in the garden, growing under standard roses, mixed with daffodils for extending the flowering season, and in dedicated beds. There is the light blue bearded iris 'Flare', the true blue 'Pension', the mauve and purple 'Heather Blush', and the dark 'Evening in Paris'. 'Plant iris rhizomes where the sun can bake them and the frost can bite them,' quips Sandy.

One of several impressive elements at The Price of Peace is the perfect lawn. Created from 'Arad' seed, a mixture of broadleaf and fine fescue grasses, it survives through summers which reach over 40°C, is said to require less water and mowing, is tough and will also grow in the shade.

From the lawn, the visitor reaches an exciting 'herb room' created by a hedge of honey myrtle (*Melaleuca armillaris*) and floored with a chequerboard of cement pavers set with a variety of thymes. 'We started off with three different types,' says Sandy. Her favourite is a cultivar of the creeping thyme which goes by the name of 'Magic Carpet' and is covered in summer with tiny white flowers. 'I designed this room by fiddling one night with a pencil and paper,' she adds.

The herb floor is encircled by a deep border of peonies; there are groupings of pinks, then reds, and then whites. 'I've gone berserk with the herbaceous peonies,' Sandy admits. 'I bought them from a grower in Tasmania who made me promise never to call them peony *roses*.'

The Price of Peace also reflects Russell's love of Australian native plants. 'My father had a conventional garden of buffalo lawn, privet hedges and roses, which means in the Sydney climate you're mowing and clipping every weekend. I read Betty Malony's *Designing Australian Bush Gardens*, which introduced me to the world of *Leptospermum*, *Acacias*, *Grevilleas* and *Banksias*.' A favourite tree is the native frangipani. 'It's covered in highly scented flowers from August to January,' says Russell. 'It doesn't seem to need a lot of water and is frost hardy.'

'Your garden is you,' says Sandy. 'To me it's like painting a picture. To get someone else in to do your garden is to me like putting your name on someone else's picture.'

Above: *Iris* 'Heather Blush' and the *Iris* 'Supreme Sultan'.

The Glen

Charles Shann chose his property, The Glen, outside Warwick in Queensland, because it reminded him of his mother's home, Maryvale, 160 kilometres north of Charters Towers.

His family were pioneers in far north Queensland, having moved north from the well-known Coolart (or Coolort, as it is written in the family diaries) on Victoria's Mornington Peninsula. His great grandfather on his mother's side, the explorer William Hann, took up Maryvale in 1861, and named it after his wife, Mary (née Hearn). 'In those days, before there was a Townsville or a Charters Towers, they had to grow all their own vegetables,' he says. 'While I'm sure there was some sort of flower garden, they largely concentrated on growing things to eat.'

Charles' grandmother was the first white child born in the far north, in 1868, and the property remains in his mother's family. 'She had a large rose garden in a 4-acre garden,' he says. 'She loved plants and would buy bulbs from the south. She terraced the garden which contained beautifully pruned citrus trees—there was a marvellous terrace of cumquats.'

After Charles Shann bought The Glen in 1977, two trips were needed to transport his collection of plants before his family arrived. When his wife, the artist Rowan Shann, saw the property, she burst into tears. 'I thought "Oh heavens, she hates it. What have I done?"' says Charles, 'until Rowan said, "You said it was beautiful, but you didn't say it was as beautiful as this." The flats were all green—it really did look beautiful,' recalls Charles.

While the stone house had been moved to the site in about 1890, there was no garden when Betty Graham had bought the property with her husband in the 1940s. Betty Graham had worked with the Victorian designer Edna Walling from 1928 to 1932, and recalled for Charles Shann, 'Walling would take off her hat, flick it round and say "Well, that's the dusting".'

It was Betty Graham who first terraced 1 hectare for the garden, and who built the stone walls that now form its bones. A trellis covered with a massive example of the yellow, single-flowered rose 'Mermaid', remains as the surviving example of her planting. Charles Shann added extensively to the size of the garden, the stonework, the design and planting and The Glen is now home to over 700 roses.

The formal rose garden—a marvellous collection of intensely-coloured 'moderns' which includes 'Peter Frankenfeld', 'Oklahoma', 'Kronenbourg' and 'Bob Woolley'—is a square, bound by beautiful stone walls. A circle in its midst houses the salmon-pink 'Duet', which is surrounded with icebergs. The roses are underplanted with rare bulbs—*Sparaxis grandiflora acutiloba*, *Ixia conferta*, *Gladiolus tristis* and *Dipidax triqueta*. 'Charles designed the rose garden by eye—by climbing on the roof and drawing it from that perspective,' says his wife.

You leave the formal rose garden by a path hedged with 'Iceberg' on one side. On the other side is a trellis of the roses 'Sparrieshoop' and 'Iceberg'—a mass of pink and white blooms.

Close by, the walls of the tennis court are covered, in that typical country way, in roses; there is the blush-pink 'New Dawn', red 'Firefall' and cream-coloured 'Sea Foam'.

A hedge of 'Bloomfield Abundance', which is sometimes confused with 'Cecile Brunner', leads off into the paddocks—the property breeds roan Droughtmaster cattle, and goats—and into the quintessential Australian landscape.

Opposite: A misty morning at The Glen.

Below: Betty Graham built the stone walls that now form the garden's bones.

Bottom left: The formal rose garden.

How this garden works

* The garden has survived various droughts by the regular use of lawn clippings. Goat manure is applied in early spring, just every three years—too much would result in an iron deficiency.

* 'Roses need a regular spray program,' says Charles Shann, 'as well as regular feeding of a good compost of manures, grass clippings and fallen leaves.'

* Charles Shann prunes in the first week of August—about six weeks before a garden opening for the hybrid teas, five weeks prior for miniatures. If there is to be an autumn garden event, he gives the roses a light prune about seven weeks before.

Russelldown Garden and Rare Poultry

Chooks are Lynne Russell's passion. Not just any chooks mind you, but chooks that are works of art. At Russelldown Garden and Rare Poultry, there are chooks with the whitest of feathers that are laced with the blackest of flecks; a brown rooster sports rich, shining, deep russet-coloured feathers with black 'whooshes' that appear to have been created by the calligrapher's pen and ink.

Being able to keep poultry must be just one of many advantages of living outside the city. The space to create a beautiful garden of over 2 hectares, with superb views over Victoria's Otway Ranges, is definitely another plus for Lynne and her husband David.

'When we bought our 5 hectares a little over a decade ago, the garden around the house had magnificent gum trees but little else,' says Lynne. 'Most of the topsoil had been removed, leaving only clay and gravel just 2 centimetres down. After copious amounts of chook manure, compost, straw and anything else we could get our hands onto, the garden beds are now well built up.'

The garden is landscaped in a series of terraces, retained by massive stone walls built by Lynne, and now softened by hedges of French and English lavender and massed, groundcover roses. 'We carted in five semi-trailer loads of rocks to build the walls,' says Lynne. Sleepers and

pylons from the old Port Arlington Pier have also been used in retaining walls and have been made into seats by David.

Lynne also admits to a passion for roses. Her favourite is the American Polyantha rose 'Pinkie', bred in 1947, which bears trusses of rose-pink flowers in spring and early summer and on, into winter. A long walkway of 100 climbing 'Pinkie' is an amazing sight in early summer and leads the visitor down to a large dam at the base of the vista.

A bow-tie shaped garden is packed with 'Iceberg' roses, and under-planted with strawberries, borage and wild violets to flower into winter. In each corner are 'weepers' of the cream rose 'Sea Foam'—probably the best rose for standardising. Another arch covered in the climbing form of 'Sea Foam', and edged with French lavender, leads from this garden.

Throughout the garden is a collection of every variety of rose bred by Englishman David Austin which is available in Australia. Among Lynne's favorites are the apricot-coloured 'Abraham Darby', the delicate 'Sweet Juliet', the remontant 'Lucetta' and the pale yellow 'The Pilgrim'.

Mass plantings of sweetly scented citrus trees and climbing, old fashioned roses camouflage the poultry pens. Russelldown is home to over 15 different breeds of poultry which share the garden with children, dogs, peacocks, cats, ducks, Chinese and Sebastopol geese, and possums which are so well fed that they don't eat the roses! Lynne's guineafowl have been road-tested on television! The collection of poultry includes the extremely rare 'Houdan', the 'Polish' with its giant 'pom pom', the 'Seabright', and the popular 'Sussex' and 'Rhode Island Red', the fluffy 'Silkie' and the 'Araucana', which lays blue eggs.

To all those who dream of collecting fresh eggs, still warm, for the morning omelette, Lynne Russell advises, 'Select your poultry like selecting a plant. It's not always the 'pretties' which will be the best for you. Buy the type of bird that best suits your conditions. Some breeds are flighty and will stray, while some breeds are happy in a small pen. For people in the city, the 'Sussex' and the 'Rhode Island Red' are best, as they are quiet. The 'Silkie' is a smaller bird that children will love and that won't dig up the garden. The 'Pekin' and the 'Bearded Belgium' are very special.'

Opposite: At Russelldown Garden and Rare Poultry, there are chooks with the whitest feathers and the blackest of flecks.

Top left: *Rosa* 'The Pilgrim'.

Top right: *Rosa* 'Abraham Darby'.

How this garden works

* Other favourite roses that cover pergolas at Russelldown include the once-flowering 'Albertine', with long pointed pink buds and wicked thorns, and 'Blossomtime'. Both are underplanted with masses of self-seeded scabiosa, or pin-cushion plant.

* The Allardii lavender (*Lavandula* x *allardii*) will do better than other species in frost-prone areas, and lavenders love lime.

* If you want to keep poultry in the city, Lynne Russell advises ringing your local council, as rules change with each ward. Some councils don't allow roosters.

Once a Jolly Farmer

I t's a long time since the busy days when horse-drawn coaches arrived in a cloud of dust at the Jolly Farmer's gate, a convict-built 1826 rest house at Perth in northern Tasmania, then on the main road between Longford and Launceston. The coaching house was built by a Mr McKinnon, probably named Jolly Farmer by its second owner, and operated until the end of the last century.

Today, Jolly Farmer is owned by well-known artist and antique dealer, Michael McWilliams. The garden that surrounds a series of wonderful buildings is almost 1 hectare, and provides plenty of inspiration and subject material for McWilliams' paintings, which depict rural scenes, gardens, animals, flowers and fruit.

The property is now set in a peaceful cul-de-sac; the only noise comes from the colourful menagerie of poultry and animals that forms a vital part of daily life at Jolly Farmer. Apart from two labradors, an Airedale and a three-legged new canine arrival, there is a collection of poultry that includes silver laced wyndotte, gold laced wyndotte, silver spangled Hamburghs, guineafowls and ducks which roam the garden. A Cape Barren goose, an Australian breed from Cape Barren Island between Tasmania and the mainland, rare and until recently an endangered species, has just been added to the collection. The poultry are chosen for their attractiveness. 'They all lay eggs,' says McWilliams, somewhat dryly.

As you push open the garden gate, you are greeted, in early summer, by a sweeping border of English lavender and blue lupins. Roses are popular in this garden; McWilliams' favourite rose is the David Austin-bred 'Graham Thomas', named after the great British rosarian. 'I love the colour, which is very rich, almost gold,' he says. In this country it grows much more vigorously than in the United Kingdom, often behaving here as a climber. A mass of the vigorous pink rose, the repeat-flowering 'Ballerina', cascades from a peach tree in front of a marvellous 1826 barn. The luscious, marshmallow-coloured rose 'Ophelia' clambers over a beautiful shed which is built from salvaged timber and bricks, ensuring that it looks original, rather than just 30 years old. The upstairs section of this building is McWilliams' studio, while the ground floor is being converted into a gallery to be opened in 2000.

This area of old buildings is separated from the vegetable garden by a dry stone wall, built recently by a local stonemason from the basalt of the area. If you walk on, a wide lawn opens to double perennial borders, filled with delphiniums and peonies, iris and day lilies. McWilliams likes the old fashioned favourites such as aquilegias, lupins and foxgloves. 'I plant shrubs in the background of a border and fill the gaps with perennials,' he says. McWilliams doesn't set out to use any particular colour schemes in the garden, and there is no one colour that is banned at Jolly Farmer. Colours are chosen that go together, 'to a

point, but sometimes it is just a combination of foliage,' he says. 'The garden's more about foliage. I'm not so fussy about flowers.'

Different parts of the garden are hidden from immediate view by plantings of shrubs; narrow paths dissect deep beds to allow for easy access. One of the many elements that contribute to making this beautiful garden so satisfying is the balance between dense planting and open lawn space, created with the advantage of an artist's sense of scale.

Opposite: Jolly Farmer was built by convicts in 1826 at Perth, in northern Tasmania.

Above: The luscious, marshmallow-coloured rose 'Ophelia'.

Left: Colours are chosen that go together, but sometimes it is just a combination of foliage.

Melbourne's Royal Botanic Gardens

n the centre of a city of almost 4 million people, and a 10-minute walk from the midst of the business district, is a garden of 35 hectares that has been acclaimed by various experts as among the greatest examples in the world of the eighteenth-century landscape style.

I write, of course, of Melbourne's Royal Botanic Gardens, credited largely to the landscape architect William Robert Guilfoyle, director of the Gardens from 1873 to 1909. He was greatly influenced by the sweeping, romantic landscapes of the eighteenth century English masters, William Kent, 'Capability' Brown—who created the dramatic landscape of Blenheim Castle—and Humphrey Repton, although Guilfoyle created his landscapes on a more intimate scale and favoured an element of surprise in his plans. After the classical formality of the seventeenth century, Kent had advocated that perspective, light and shade were all important, adding that 'nature abhors a straight line'.

The influence of Guilfoyle's plant hunting expeditions to the Pacific Islands is also seen in areas of the Gardens such as the fern gully, where the eighteenth century romantic landscape is overlaid with the nineteenth century Paradise style—the visitor enters a paradise which isn't quite real. 'The paintings of Rousseau come to mind,' says the current Director, Dr Philip Moors.

Born in England on 8 December, 1840, William Guilfoyle was the eldest son of a horticultural family that arrived in Sydney in the late 1840s. After opening a nursery at Redfern, his father, Michael, was commissioned to landscape Greenoaks, the Darling Point property of the merchant Thomas Mort. Guilfoyle senior then opened a much-admired nursery on three-and-a-half acres in Double Bay, and was involved in the landscaping of Sydney's Botanic Gardens and Domain.

William Guilfoyle was pioneering the sugarcane industry in northern New South Wales when he was invited to become curator of the Melbourne Gardens. He nursed a grand vision, assisted by the wealth of the city at the time; Melbourne was entering its golden period and there were few financial restrictions on Guilfoyle's vision and genius.

While the Gardens are very much pleasure grounds, they are also of enormous botanical significance—there are 50 000 individual plants of some 12 000 species, from all parts of the world. Part of Guilfoyle's design was the incorporation of water interest; he took advantage of an alteration to the course of the Yarra River to create, from what was marshy, swampy land, the Ornamental Lake which is central to the life of the Gardens. Around the Lake, Guilfoyle's brilliance is very much in evidence. Plant material is arranged in layers, from ground covers up, with different textures and leaf shapes accentuating the effect.

At the top of the Hopetoun Lawn are the last vestiges of the pinetum, the work of the previous and first director, Baron Ferdinand von Mueller. It was to here that Guilfoyle came when he wanted mature trees with which to create the apices of his vistas. He would dig up large pines and move them from one area of the garden to another with the help of horse-drawn vehicles.

Many will empathise with Philip Moors when he says he has 'the most special job in Melbourne—to be able to work and walk through such a wonderful landscape is indeed a privilege'.

Left: The rose 'Mister Lincoln'.

Rymill Winery

They've been growing grapes in the red soil of the beautiful Coonawarra district of South Australia for more than 100 years, but it's perhaps only over the last couple of decades that the area has developed into a centre for wine and food lovers and has drawn thousands of visitors to its arts festival, held each May.

Summertime finds the area also showing off its rose gardens. As well as the splendid rose gardens at wineries such as Balnaves and Kidmans, each winery has chosen a particular rose to create living fences and to plant at the end of each row of vines.

At the Rymill Winery, situated some 15 kilometres north of the township of Penola, it's the deep red hybrid tea 'Mr Lincoln'. 'It's deliciously fragrant and wonderful to pick,' says Andrew Rymill. 'Tradition has it that diseases show up on the roses before being noticeable in the denser canopy of the vines. Also, the roses at the end of the rows were a visual marker for the horses before the days of mechanisation, to discourage them from cutting across and knocking over the last post of the row.'

The Rymill family has been in the area since the nineteenth century; Andrew Rymill and his brother Peter are the great grandsons of John Riddoch, acknowledged as the father of the Coonawarra. Riddoch was born in 1827 in Scotland, the son of a farmer; he was 23 years old when he arrived in Victoria on an assisted passage. He soon struck gold at the Ovens Valley diggings, and within two years had established himself as a wholesale wine and general merchant in Geelong. He married fellow migrant Elizabeth King, buying Yallum, near Penola, in 1861, a run eventually expanded to 50 000 hectares, supporting 110 000 sheep and 3000 cattle. Their youngest daughter Mary married Robert Rymill, the neighbouring farmer at Penola Station, in 1902; Mary and Robert's son was John, also renowned as the arctic explorer.

His son, Peter, has developed the Riddoch Run Vineyards since 1974, planting out some 80 hectares by 1994. The Rymill Winery operation started in 1990 and the present building was completed in November 1995. The pair of fighting stallions in front of the winery, cast in bronze by Dutch-born artist Gabriel Sterk, reflect the Rymill family's, and the region's, deep involvement with horses.

The garden at the winery is reminiscent, perhaps, of parts of France, with the clean lines of the marvellous building echoed in the straight rows of vines and in the windbreaks of Lombardy poplars and cypress. An avenue of oriental plane (*Platanus orientalis*) leads into the winery. 'They're more compact and easily trained than London plane,' says Andrew. 'And of course we've followed the French tradition with those roses at the end of the rows of vines.'

Above: Stunning lines at the Rymill Winery.

Ellensbrook

We all know our pioneering women were extraordinary, that they came, often, from gentle backgrounds of soft and misted English climates to summers of snakes, flies, mosquitoes and century heat that seems to burn off the eyelids.

It's surely difficult to imagine today just how strong and enterprising these colonial women were—and the early settlers of Western Australia must be among our most courageous. Twenty-four-year-old Georgiana Molloy, one of the first settlers to brave the wild south-western coast, wrote, after the death of her baby, born after her arrival at Augusta in a tent under an umbrella held against the driving rain, 'language refuses to utter what I experienced when mine died in my arms in this dreary land'.

Arriving in Perth with Molloy on the *Warrior* in March 1830 were the Bussell brothers, including the youngest, Alfred, who was to marry 16-year-old Ellen Heppingstone in 1850.

Alfred and Ellen, led by an Aboriginal guide from the local Wardandi tribe, arrived at the inaccessible Ellensbrook site in 1857, with their three tiny daughters. The isolated coastal setting, just south of today's township of Margaret River, was chosen because of the supply of fresh, running water.

During the eight years that Ellen and Alfred Bussell were at Ellensbrook, they established a dairy and beef cattle farm with the crucial help of the Aborigines. As they farmed the coastal heath, no clearing was involved, and they quickly became self-sufficient, with vegetable gardens, a huge potato patch and cereal and grain crops. Their wheat field was within 100 metres of the Indian Ocean. Ellen also created substantial decorative gardens which are to be restored.

The wattle and daub section of Ellen and Alfred's five-room house was built between 1857 and 1860. They had two more daughters at Ellensbrook, two sons and raised two Aboriginal children, including Sam Isaacs, who wandered in as a six-year-old and later became head stockman. (It was Isaacs who, in 1876, rode into the sea with 16-year-

old Grace Bussell to rescue some 60 people from the *Georgette* as the ship foundered on rocks on the treacherous coast.)

Alfred Bussell was much involved in politics, in the development of the timber industry and with the establishment of what is now the Bussell Highway. The spirit of calm strength that pervades Ellensbrook today recalls the extraordinary women who created and ran the property.

The repeated tragedy that was so common to early settlers persuaded Ellen and Alfred to leave Ellensbrook, after eight years and the deaths of their two infant sons. Their eldest daughter, 20-year-old Fanny, took over the property in 1871. By 1877 she had added two stone rooms to the house, and had developed the farm to hold 200 head of stock. Her diary records the building of cattle pens, fences, a dairy and a churnhouse. At 19, Fanny had married John Brockman, whose shipping ventures twice resulted in the loss of the Ellensbrook stock, furniture and fittings. After the death of her mother at 43, leaving the thirteenth child, Filumena, just months old, Fanny, who never had her own children, moved to look after her family at nearby Walcliffe House.

Edith, the second daughter, took over Ellensbrook that year and ran the farm, alone, for 40 years, and from 1899 to 1917, ran the property as a home for Aboriginal children.

Ellensbrook, situated in the Leeuwin–Naturaliste National Park, among the peppermint trees and within a unique and beautiful landscape that remains unchanged since the days of Ellen and Alfred Bussell, is today in the care of the National Trust.

The manager, John Summers, has succeeded in maintaining perfectly the grounds and the house, while retaining Ellensbrook's unique and moving spirit. 'It's a powerful place both for those of European background and for Aboriginal people,' he says. 'So many people feel an instant connection and feel the power. This is a great example of what could have been for Aboriginal people and the new settlers. The descendants of Ngili, who was raised here, still come regularly to reconnect with the positive spirit of the place. I draw upon it daily.'

Opposite and left: Ellensbrook is situated in the Leeuwin–Naturaliste National Park, among the peppermint trees and within a unique and beautiful landscape.

The Grampians

Victoria's western district is home to a great collection of marvellous gardens, many of which you can visit and in many of which you can stay. There are wonderful rose gardens, important botanic gardens and historic homesteads with beautiful gardens that are more than a century old.

The area is also nature's garden, providing endless walks across fields of wildflowers, or climbs into the Grampians. Wherever you walk, or drive, this rugged mountain range with its razor-sharp façades and its luminescent blue presence, seems to dominate. The garden designer Edna Walling was devoted to the Grampians, not just because they provided the most perfect background to any garden picture, but also because of their grandeur. She wrote, however, in her very collectable *A Gardener's Log*, published in 1948, that 'for all their magnificence they're so friendly'. Walling described her delight when, after climbing 'up and up', she came 'face to face with thousands of Baeckias and the shell-pink Boronia. I just sat down and gazed and gazed. To have seen anything so exquisitely beautiful before one dies seemed to be all that mattered!'

In *The Australian Roadside*, first published in 1952, Edna Walling called the Grampians 'the site of one of the loveliest natural flower gardens in Australia'.

You don't have to climb to enjoy clouds of wildflowers in the district. A 20-minute stroll at the southern foot of the Grampians, close to the village of Dunkeld, with Mount Abrupt a constant companion, will take you across a landscape of the grass tree, *Xanthorrhoea australis*, flowering from September to December and a white carpet of Victorian smoke bush, *Conospermum mitchelli*, which is endemic to the sandy woodland and heathland of the area.

The Dunkeld and Hamilton visitor information centres, situated on the largest volcanic plain in the Southern Hemisphere, can assist visitors to the southern Grampians with expert information. Extremely knowledgeable local volunteers can tell you, for instance, that Mount Eccles is an absolute jewel and is home to a large colony of koalas.

Top left: The grass tree, *Xanthorrhoea australis*.

Top right: The Victorian smoke bush, *Conospermum mitchelli*.

Scent

Many years ago, I met a charming English businessman. Whenever after he came to Australia he would bring me a bottle of a fragrance called Fracas—still my favourite and, some would say, aptly named. 'Oh what lovely perfume,' said I, upon receiving this gift on the first occasion. 'Scent, my dear,' he said gravely. 'You are sold perfume. You wear scent.'

Scent, fragrance, perfume, as we all know, is evocative of so much. The scent of a certain perfume can remind you of a friend you haven't seen for years; the fragrance of a certain suntan oil can place you on Surfers beach and take you back to the summer you learned to waterski.

The smell of beeswax can evoke a most comfortable sense of security as it conjures up old houses filled with well-tended furniture. On the other hand, the smell of coffee in David Jones always causes a twinge of fear as it recalls the memory of wicked and surreptitious dashes into the food hall although admonished to travel straight back to school from the dentist.

You know Christmas is around the corner when the large-flowered gardenia blooms. It only takes one flower to fill the house with the most delicious fragrance; the scent can transport you back to childhood and the picture of the Christmas table set with these fragile white flowers.

The smaller the garden, the harder each plant must work. You can fit a lot of pleasure into a small place if you follow the dictate that everything you own should be either beautiful or useful. That's scented plants for you—both beautiful and useful. A courtyard garden of clipped hedges restraining a variety of gardenias—G. 'Radicans' for groundcover, 'Professor Pucci' forming the next layer and the tall-growing G. 'Magnifica' to shut out the city grind, will provide weeks of joy. Perhaps the very best scent of all is that of the citrus, with the inauspicious blossom thrilling you with the intensity of her fragrance.

A single *Magnolia denudata* will fill a small garden with its scent toward the end of winter. You can't go past the bull bay magnolia (*M. grandiflora*) if you have a garden large enough to allow the tree to spread. Perhaps like all true beauties, this magnolia is somewhat elusive; as soon as you pick her, she fades. She performs from Tasmania to Townsville, flowering in summer and filling the air with her divine fragrance.

In a cold climate garden, the excitement starts toward the end of winter with the *Daphne odora*—could this be the greatest scent of all?

Then come the viburnums, especially *V. carlesii*, the favourite of that English gardening legend, Vita Sackville-West, whose glorious garden, Sissinghurst, still excites and amazes, unfazed and unspoilt by millions of words of reverence from an adoring public.

Below: The lilac *Syringa vulgaris* 'Mme Lemoine'.

Bottom: The scent of summer is petunias.

Colour companions

English photographer and garden writer Andrew Lawson was in Australia in 1998 conducting garden photography workshops and lecturing on his pet subject, colour in the garden. Through his pictures, he showed how colours can be matched or contrasted, how tones of the one colour can be used to great effect and how a small splash of one colour can provide the shock needed to prevent boredom.

At Helen and Kenneth Neale's historic property, Blackdown, built west of the Blue Mountains in 1823 for Elizabeth and Thomas Hawkins, the main perennial border is dominated by mauves, purples and blues, accentuated with the black iris 'Blackout'. The lilac flowers of *Hesperis matronalis* are scented in the summer evenings; the marvellous glaucous-

with-pinks foliage of *Melianthus major* tones with the cream and bruised-pink catkins of *Garrya elliptica*. The earthy colours of chocolate cosmos offset the purple-leaved smoke bush and the plum-coloured *Heuchera* 'Palace Purple'. Glamour is introduced with the single oriental poppy 'Blackdown Purple', grown from seed sent by the Royal Horticultural Society. Andrew Lawson's favourite poppy 'Patty's Plum' would add further drama—if one of our enterprising specialist nurserymen were to import it. The rare and charming, black-leaved *Geranium sessiliflorum* 'Nigricans' would also go well, planted at the front of the border.

The colour wash against which these divas perform is provided by the grey-leaved plants, which Helen feels are essential to lift the palette of intense colours, as well as to allow the eye to rest. There are tanacetums, as well as *Salvia argentea* and the essential *Artemisia* 'Powis Castle'. Pizazz is injected with the crushed-raspberry colours of the sweet pea 'Cupani', which was rediscoverd in an old garden at Bathurst and is now growing in the Royal Botanic Gardens in Sydney. 'And I adore the teasels—they have the lovely foliage which is so important in a border, beautiful purple flowers, and then marvellous seed pods,' says Helen Neale.

Colour harmonies create peace in any garden. One of the first clematis to flower after winter, *C.* 'Fair Rosamund', teams perfectly with *Wisteria sinensis* 'Alba', which flowers at the same time. The long white-flushed-with-pink racemes of the wisteria tone with the pale cream outer petals and burgundy stamens of the clematis. Add the spring-flowering tall bearded iris 'Imprimis', or 'Conch Call' and enjoy the compliments.

Good luck can lead to some happy flirtations: the stripe on the buds of *Rosa* 'Mme Gregoire Staechelin' matches perfectly the *Clematis* 'Red Corona' that you may have selected in the nursery as it was the only one in flower. Such success may lead to further adventures: the old tea rose, 'Baronne Henriette de Snoy', the colour of aged, crushed silk, looks marvellous planted in the border with the effortless bronze-leaved fennel. The red stems of the rose pick up the deep pink 'eye' in Andrew Lawson's recommended lupin 'The Chatelaine'.

The early spring green leaves of the silver birch are the perfect foil for the apricot flowers of the climbing rose 'Leonie Vienot'. The lemon colour in both the rose and the birch leaves make the combination charming.

Colour contrasts provide a different kind of excitement. The bright golden yellow leaves of the *Hosta* 'August Moon' are in perfect counterpoint with the deep red of *Acer palmatum* 'Crimson Queen'.

Perhaps it is the realisation that we are all artists when we garden that makes us somewhat obsessive. You don't have to be acclaimed to notice that the pink splashes on the leaves of *Acer palmatum* 'Oridono-nishiki' are echoed by a mass of the pastel-striped soft grass *Phalaris* 'Feesey' and an underplanting of *Epimedium* x *rubrum*, or that the addition of the bright pink flowers of *Achillea* 'The Beacon' will add drama and prevent complacency.

Opposite: The historic property, Blackdown, was built west of the Blue Mountains in 1823.

Above: *Clematis* 'Red Corona'.

Left: The sweet pea 'Cupani'.

How this garden works

* Use a dash of red in a border of tones of yellows or blues. *Geum* 'Mrs Bradshaw' is an exciting clear red.

* The white-edged *Hosta* 'Thomas Hogg' or *H.* 'Francee' emerges at the same time as the lacy white flowers bloom along the layered branches of *Viburnum plicatum*.

* Taking 'happy snaps' of your garden is the best way to evaluate and refine: the eye is focussed, not distracted by all else that is happening. Mistakes, as well as opportunities, are more obvious.

Windy city

Gardeners are often troubled over the choice between a wonderful view and the need to provide plants with some protection from damaging winds. When Robyn Cameron moved to her hilltop garden, Langleigh, outside Walcha on the Northern Tablelands of New South Wales, just four years ago, she was faced with such a dilemma.

Windbreaks had to be planted immediately and each tree had to be staked. 'The most severe winds come from the south west,' says Robyn. A double row of Leyland cypress (x *Cupressocyparis leylandii* 'Leighton's Green') was planted about 10 metres behind the house, to the south. To the west of the house another stand of cypress was planted with a row of *Photinia robusta* in front. This layering of plants filters the wind, instead of channelling it to move with equal force in another direction.

Similarly, copses of trees are planted throughout the garden to further break up the wind.

'Each tree had to be staked,' says Robyn. 'Particularly the whippy trees like the birches or robinias.' The stakes could be removed after three years for the more solid trees like the oaks and elms. 'You can't use twine, which will cut into the tree,' says Robyn. 'We use old car tubes, cut and wrapped around the wires which are attached to stakes on three sides to hold the tree firm against the wind.'

When deciding where the trees will be planted, preserving as much of the stunning view as possible, stakes are hammered into the ground and left for a couple of weeks to ensure the site is correct. Large copses of fast-growing natives have been planted as 'nursery trees', protecting

3 metres in diameter and are backed with a tapestry of smoke bush, berberis, may, viburnums and lilacs, all protected by the now dense hedges of cypress.

Massive quantities of gypsum have been needed to break down the clay soil. Robyn is a lucky gardener, however. She and her husband Gordon grow lucerne on the beautiful river flats which the house over looks. Occasionally, the river floods and Robyn is the grateful recipient of bales of spoiled lucerne hay which is applied in thick layers around each tree to preserve moisture.

Beyond the plantings around the house is a thicket of sacred bamboo (*Nandina domestica*), both for protection and also to divide the outer part of the garden, which is left in a more natural state. Here a woodland of trees only needs to be mown twice a year.

Throughout the paddocks, Robyn has planted groups of trees, all protected from the cattle by carefully constructed tree guards. There are English elm (*Ulmus procera*), pin oak (*Quercus palustris*) and tulip trees (*Liriodendron tulipifera*). Along the road Robyn has planted copses of poplars (*Populus nigra* 'Italica') which colour wonderfully in autumn. There are also golden elm (*Ulmus procera* 'Louis van Houtte') planted just outside the house fence to link the outside with the golden elm planted in the garden.

The eye then brings the surroundings up to the house and the breathtaking landscape becomes part of the garden.

Opposite: The lovely hilltop garden of Langleigh outside Walcha on the Northern Tablelands of New South Wales.

Left: Drifts of snow-in-summer and convolvulus cascade down the retaining wall.

young 'exotics' from frost and snow. A favourite in this harsh climate is the snow gum, *Eucalyptus pauciflora* var. *niphophila*, with its beautiful bark of whites, carmine and greens.

The low house, which nestles into the ground, has been built on a flat, excavated site; a massive bank has been created behind, as further protection from the wind. This has been retained by sawn telephone posts kept in place by upright steel posts. Robyn's discipline in choosing just a few different types of very hardy plants has been very successful here; the result has been a quick and glamorous groundcover. Drifts of snow-in-summer and convolvulus cascade down the retaining wall. Plantings of catmint, iris, penstemons and lavenders are now each

How this garden works

* Filter the wind. Take care when creating windbreaks of plant material or shade cloth not to create a tunnel for the wind or a barrier over which the wind can be dumped on the garden.

* Wooden stakes are sufficient for smaller trees, while larger trees need steel posts.

* Mulch is the key to success in any garden, particularly where water can be scarce. Use anything you can get your hands on; if using spoiled lucerne hay, the second cut will be weed free.

All I want for Christmas . . .

You are driving behind a car that is travelling infuriatingly slowly. What is wrong with that woman, you think, aloud and impatiently, as her vehicle inches along at a fragile pace. Is she suffering from sleep deprivation? Perhaps she has a newborn baby? Is she talking on her mobile phone? Is she running out of petrol? No, the truth will be that yet again, and against her better judgment, she has succumbed to the temptation of buying an orchid. She is now trying to reach home without damaging its delicate, moth-like blooms.

This brings us to Christmas which, as we are suddenly, shockingly aware, 'is just around the corner'. High on every gardener's Christmas wish list is, surely, an orchid that is guaranteed to flower more than the once, on the occasion upon which it was purchased. The perfect gardening glove, a trowel that won't bend nor break and a load of aged manure would also be high on the list for many gardeners.

Some good advice on the care of orchids might be the next-best gift to the ever-blooming orchid. Marcelle Collee of Honeysuckle Gardens nursery in Sydney's Bondi Junction says, 'Orchids like to be root bound, so only repot them every two years. Water once a week and drain; they are epiphytes, so don't leave them standing in a saucer. After they've flowered, place them outside, under a deciduous tree, not in direct sun.' She advises fertilising *Phalaenopsis* orchids from February with flower-inducing fertiliser. 'When flowering is finished use a growth fertiliser. And to prevent fungal infection, keep water off leaves.'

Photographer Lorna Rose's favourite orchid is the *Phalaenopsis* species. 'They are so graceful.' She adores photographing plants with intriguing markings and complex structures. 'The species orchid from Vietnam, *Cirrhopetalum fascinator*, fits the bill,' she says. 'It has long thread-like tails hanging from purple spotted blooms.' The Columbian orchid *Restrepia antennifera*, is another favourite. 'It's a rich yellow covered in leopard-like red spots. But interesting detail can be seen in all plants,' says Rose. 'It's just a case of taking the time to look.'

A garden journal, to record what precious bulb has been planted where so that you won't later murder it with a spade, could be high on the Christmas list. Several pairs of effective gardening gloves, like the rubber-coated gloves by Twiggs, are another must for Christmas. The perfect trowel was always high on my list of wants, but now Longreach Garden Tools has invented the multi-use *Trovell*; they also make beautiful leather gloves for pruning and picking roses.

Lorna Rose would like lightweight secateurs that are self-sharpening and cleaning under her Christmas tree. To me, a load of aged manure, delivered, would be pretty special.

However, if on Christmas Day I find a garden heavy with the scent of gardenia, a table surrounded by happy children and the conversation of family and friends, I'll be more than content.

Left: A soft-stem dendrobium and a king orchid cling to a leopard tree at *Shady Tree,* the Buderim garden of Michael Collins Persse.

Boxed in

Polly and Peter Park's 30-year-old garden, Boxford, comprises six different worlds, all set in a quiet, leafy, Canberra street.

The Parks acknowledge the influence of the great designer and writer Russell Page and the Brazilian designer and artist Roberto Burle Marx. 'Both said that the overall picture must have a focal point with everything relating to that point,' explains Polly Park.

The late Roberto Burle Marx is considered by many as the greatest landscape architect of our time. 'He was classic but also innovative,' says Polly. 'He said that everything should be planted in volumes—he recommended using just one type of plant or just one colour.'

Upon arrival at Boxford you notice immediately the immaculate hedges of box (*Buxus sempervirens* 'Suffruticosa'), underplanted with massed periwinkle (*Vinca minor*), which was chosen as it doesn't take over as does the larger-flowered *Vinca major*.

The visitor moves from one mood to another, through the different garden compartments, each reflecting the travels of the owners. Japanese visitors come here to meditate in the peace of the Japanese garden, with its 300-year-old stone lantern, granite water bowl and bamboo ladle.

The most compelling part of the garden for many visitors is the parterre garden, which is enclosed by a fence supporting ivy, trained in a method which dates to Roman times. This wonderfully effective method entails attaching wires in a diamond pattern and planting the ivy at the base. Just one strand of each plant is allowed to grow and is twisted around the wire. When the ivy reaches the desired height it is allowed to spread to become a hedge along the top of the fence.

This unique area is divided into four beds, each quarter home to a weeping cherry (*Prunus* 'Mount Fuji'), underplanted again with the periwinkle and edged with box. The centrepiece of this garden 'room' is the delightful marble statue by Italian artist Romanelli, *circa* 1880, and bought by the owners in Florence.

Strong design is seen again in the very modern main garden, which is both flamboyant and serene. The different abstract shapes mirror each other. Magnificent tiles, brought home by the owners from Iran, Istanbul, Morocco and Portugal, are set into the white walls which surround this garden. The central feature here is a bright glass mosaic wall designed and created by Polly. The shape of the wall is reflected in the shape of the two beds, one of blue annuals, and one of white polished stones, under a spreading box elder, and in the elliptical shape of the lawn. The balance of colour, texture and shape, following the teachings of Burle Marx, is very successful. Boxford is classified as a heritage garden by the National Trust.

Above: Boxford comprises six different worlds, all set in a quiet, leafy, Canberra street.

Artistic borders

Don't plan on a fleeting visit to David Glenn's Lambley Nursery and Garden, at Ascot, near Ballarat in Victoria. The garden, which has been created around an 1870s stone farmhouse, is so full of ideas and inspiration, and David is so generous with his time, that your next appointment is likely to send out a search party.

Unlike most gardeners, who plant borders to peak in early summer, David Glenn plans so that the perennial borders at Lambley are at their peak in March. At a time of year when most of us are gasping for cool air and are dreaming of putting the garden to bed for winter, the borders at Lambley are gearing up to put on the performance of the year.

David and his artist wife, Criss Canning, moved to this hot and dry district from a very different climate in the Dandenongs some five years ago. Nature is never a push-over, and on her paintings, Criss uses up to a dozen colours to achieve just the right tone or hue to convey the feel and scent of a flower. It is Criss who designs the colour and texture of the borders and David who puts her unique treatments into play.

The huge range of plant material in the gardens at Lambley—more than 90 different genera—has set up a natural process of elimination, obviating any need for spraying for pests. 'We do get aphids in early spring, but within two weeks the ladybirds have arrived to take care of them,' says David Glenn.

Through his friendship with nurserymen around the world, David brings the latest plants into Australia to be well trialled before release through his mail-order catalogue the following year. Every new plant is put out, into the field, to test against 44°C heat in summer and –8°C temperatures in winter.

At the moment David is very excited by the heucheras. 'They are very easy, generous plants,' he says. 'They give the effect of *Astilbe*, which are much too thirsty for us. The flowers are a feathery mass, the foliage is good, and they bulk up wonderfully for a dense, well-covered border.'

Lambley offers 15 different species of *Heuchera*, including *H.* 'White Spires' which, having passed all the tests, will be released in the next few months. 'It has wonderful white spires which flower for up to three months and beautiful, dark green, crinkled leaves throughout the remainder of the year. The only attention the heucheras need is lifting and dividing in autumn every few years,' says David.

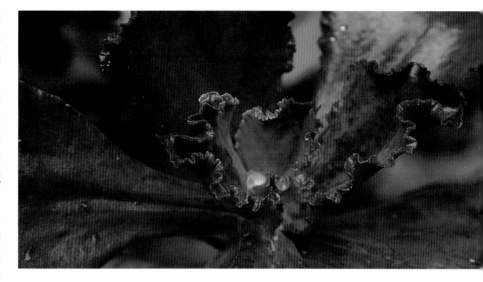

Among Lambley's collection of *Heuchera* is the just-released, black-leaved *H.* 'Amethyst', which looks marvellous in a border of grey plants including cardoons, to echo the shape of its leaves; *Artemisia* 'Powis Castle', to add softness and fullness to the scheme; *Dianthus* 'Black Night'; and *Euphorbia amygdaloides* 'Purpurea' with its black foliage and cream spires of flowers. Another find from Lambley is *Anthriscus sylvestris* 'Ravenswing', a form of the cow parsley of the English hedgerow, this one with black leaves and a delicate froth of white flowers.

David has also released the *Delphinium* 'Volkerfrieden' which arrived in Australia from the German nurseryman, Karl Foerster, who has devoted 50 years of his life to breeding plants. These branching delphiniums are self-supporting, making the time-consuming and unsightly use of staking no longer necessary.

The species *Geranium* also show their worth at this time of year, and Lambley offers a range of 30 species and cultivated varieties, including the blue-violet *Geranium* 'Criss Canning' and the bright pink *G. endressii* 'Wargrave Pink'. There is also the fashionable and useful *G. maderense*, for the back of the border; it grows very tall, is completely drought-tolerant and will also grow in complete shade.

Of increasing importance in Australian gardens are the sedums. Greatly loved at Lambley, they create interest throughout the seasons.

Opposite: *Sedum* syn 'Autumn Joy'.

Top: *Echeveria* x hybrid 'Red Edge'.

Middle: *Sedum* 'Autumn Joy'.

Right: *Sedum* 'Purple Emperor'.

Longford Hall

I f you've coveted those candelabra primula which always seem to grow in easy swathes in English gardens, the carpets of them at Rose and David Falkiner's garden, Longford Hall, will also make you envious.

The garden at Longford Hall, a sheep and crop-growing property in northern Tasmania, is set around an 1828 Georgian house, and was laid out in the early 1830s by William Tucker, a professional gardener who came to Australia at the request of Governor Arthur.

You arrive at Longford Hall through solid wooden gates supported by original brick piers and a 100-year-old topiaried box. The marvellous entrance drive is lined with over 100 metres of hawthorn and box hedging, through which the scented rose 'Meg', apricot-coloured with russet-red stamens, scrambles. The trees here have been selected for form and the arrangement of their branches. A layered tracery of leaves and branches is created by *Styrax japonica*, a beautiful tree with graceful spreading arms, and several dogwoods including *Cornus alternifolia* 'Argentea', *C. nuttallii* and *C. controversa* 'Variegata'. The 'ballerina arms' of the handkerchief tree (*Davidia involucrata*) hold hands with the Judas tree (*Cercis siliquastrum*) and the delicate, cut-leaf alders.

There is a tricolour beech (*Fagus sylvatica* 'Purpurea Tricolor'), purchased in spring to ensure that the colour of its leaves is the desirable purple, with pink margins. *Betula utilis* var. *jacquemontii*, the birch with the whitest bark, is here, with a tulip tree (*Liriodendron tulipifera*), which supports a rampaging clematis. Underneath, banks of old rhododendron, camellias and azaleas create months of bloom, scent and visual excitement.

At the top of the drive a massive oak (*Quercus robur*), planted in 1835, spreads shade over the lawn in front of the house, its leaves, composted, also making the best mulch. 'A perfect oak should be like an umbrella through which you can see to the top,' says Rose.

The garden has been designed as a series of walks. Dense shrubberies open to lawn surrounded by perennial borders. In one of several cleverly planted herbaceous borders, the tree peony 'Etienne de France' grows with a deep ruby-red rhododendron which tones with the red leaves of a *Pieris japonica*.

Nearby, is a complete collection of the English David Austin roses which are available in Australia. A walk lined with poles covered in the pink and cream French-bred climbing rose 'Pierre de Ronsard' separates this area from an expanse of lawn.

The large and intricate vegetable garden is to the left of this walk; all manner of vegetables include snow peas, runner beans and artichokes. These are interspersed with poppies and the great-value sea hollies (*Eryngium* spp.) for picking and to provide interest when the vegetables are not at their very best.

As in many of the great gardens in this area, treasured alpines are grown in home-made and very effective 'stone' pots. Rose Falkiner paints hers with yoghurt or cow manure to age them quickly.

Opposite: A terrace of old roses and clipped box.

Left: The herbaceous borders at Longford Hall house echiums, peonies and roses.

How this garden works

* When buying trees, which will become the backbone of the garden, study the form and shape of the tree and the habit of its branches—horizontal lines are so much more pleasing.

* Rose Falkiner advises choosing trees when in leaf if they are to be bought for their colour. Her marvellous tricolour beech was bought in spring; choose autumn colouring trees in autumn.

* Garden lovers who take their car on the ferry from Melbourne to Devonport can buy up at Tasmania's marvellous nurseries. Be warned—you can't take plants into Tasmania without the appropriate certificates.

Culpepper's

As we sweltered through the summer of 1997 the roses, somewhat paradoxically, or perhaps predictably, never looked better. Roses thrive on tough conditions and on dry heat, although you can also see roses growing beautifully in the humid hinterland behind the Sunshine Coast, in Queensland. At Peachester, on the Sunshine Coast, a four-year-old rose garden and nursery has been created by Julie Camillo and Barry Stowe from 'a paddock in the bush'.

For sub-tropical and temperate climates, Barry advises growing the old tea roses, the Chinas and the Bourbons, which originated from *Rosa chinensis* on the Isle de Bourbon (the island off the coast of Africa, now called Reunion) in 1817, and the Noisettes, which developed around the same time. He likes particularly the tea roses 'Duchesse de Brabant', nick-named 'the Montville rose' because it grows so well in the area, as well as 'Monsieur Tillier', 'Mrs Dudley Cross', 'Marie van Houtte', and 'General Gallieni'. Tea roses become darker in colour as they age, one of the reasons they were so popular in China in the gardens of the Mandarins.

Tea roses are easy to grow from cuttings, which avoids the infuriating problem of the rose suckering from the understock. The few teas which resist being propagated on their own roots can be grafted onto a tougher tea rootstock. At Culpepper's, the copper-pink-coloured tea 'Souvenir de Mme. Leonie Viennot' is used.

According to Barry, 'Another brilliant tea is "Safrano"—a bush can have at any one time over 400 blooms. She grows very well from cuttings, is happy in the shade and never gets black spot.'

Rosa laevigata, the 'Cherokee Rose', which arrived in America from China at the end of the eighteenth century, flowers at Culpepper's from

early September, and is grown from cuttings to form thick boundary hedges, impenetrable to wildlife.

Another group of roses suited to the Queensland climate is the hybrid musks; 'Cornelia' which enjoys the humidity and rain, has been used as hedging throughout the garden.

The favourite rose at Culpepper's is the Noisette, 'Crepuscule', an old-gold, almost thornless rose. The wonderfully scented 'Parks's Yellow', said to be the original tea rose, covers trellises throughout the garden, and comes a close second.

'The Sunshine Coast of Australia experiences dry winters, and early spring can be very stressful for the plants, before the monsoon arrives in October,' says Barry. 'We prune hard in February, so that the rose rests in the hottest part of the year. In March, Queensland experiences something of an 'English summer', with cool mornings and 20°C days. The blooms that follow are fantastic and last until July.' A light 'haircut' is given in August. Barry learnt this treatment in a similar climate in India.

Water is a problem in Queensland, so the roses have to be tough—after being nursed in their infancy, they only receive an hour-long soaking each week. Heavy mulching, and the application of lots of manure and other organic matter, is essential.

Opposite: The entrance gate, guarded by a mass of *Rosa laevigata*.

Top left: The rose 'Monsieur Tillier'.

Top right: The Noisette rose 'Alister Stella Gray' also known as 'Golden Rambler'.

How this garden works

* Fish fertiliser is used against aphids at Culpepper's. The owners change brands regularly so pests don't build up a resistance. A liquid seaweed is sprayed on the rosebushes, from early September until the end of March, once every three weeks, in the late afternoon.

Black Springs Bakery

Ten minutes down the hill from Beechworth, in the north-east of Victoria, is a cluster of beautiful stone buildings looking out over the lush rollings hills of the Buckland Valley to the indigo-blue Mount Buffalo—a view classified by the National Trust. The granite buildings, including original stables, barn and bakery, were built in about 1870 for the Price family and are set around a lawn courtyard. They have now been restored by Rob Cowell, a young garden designer who possesses more talent than is fair in one person.

Rob has restored the lovely drystone walls, unearthed paths, preserving such treasures as a classified ironbark (*Sideroxylon rosea*), and has replanted the garden with plants that require minimum water. The granite buildings have been restored, the woodwork painted with a lime wash created by Rob, and the colours of Provence have been used to create a scene also at home among the blue tints of Australian gums.

The central courtyard is planted with swathes of iris and lavender; roses and clematis grow on the grey stone walls. A fenced, decorative vegetable garden is packed with edible plants to which delphiniums, nasturtiums and sweet peas add colour. Locally-made French-style *cloches* protect young basil and tomato plants from late frosts and borders are edged with chives. Rob has planted a walkway of 20 'Smirna' quince, which leads to a seat, painted in his blue. 'I planted quince following the French country habit of everything in the garden being edible,' says Rob.

'I like the importance the French place on food for good living, so I wanted to put in plant material that is useful as well as decorative.'

Rob has planted a 0.5 hectare olive grove, the North African 'Nab Tamri' cultivar, chosen because it crops heavily and can take extremes of heat and cold. The 100 trees are planted 3 metres apart. All have plastic tree guards buried just below the surface as protection from rabbits and to preserve water. Olives need about 11 to 20 litres of water per fortnight, but heavy mulching has allowed Rob to use half this amount of water and has ensured a wonderful rate of growth. The first olive crop was harvested in the autumn of 2000 and was cured locally. Eventually a weekend to celebrate the olive will be held. The traditional method of picking the fruit by hitting the trees with sticks, along with washing, and then pressing the fruit for oil, will be demonstrated.

Olives are not fussy about soil, as long as drainage is good. As Rob's soil is over clay, he has added great quantities of gypsum and lime into each individually dug hole. The guineafowl introduced into the garden to eat the grasshoppers have proved a good deterrent against rabbits as the foxes which hunt the guineafowl turn to the rabbits, when the guineafowl elude them by resting in the trees.

These pages: The granite buildings at Black Springs Bakery, including the original stables, barn and bakery, were all built around 1870.

How this garden works

* Tree guards, bought from your local nursery, save work and heartbreak when planting young trees, as they contain a tube into which water is poured for constant moisture. They also protect against wildlife.

* Rob Cowell's easy lime wash for wood or stonework: Mix in a garbage bin 20 kilograms limsil and 1 cup skim milk powder with water to the consistency of 'skinny milk'. If mixture is not this consistency, the lime wash will dry too thick and will become hard and crack. Apply with paintbrush. Tint with water based paint to desired colour.

Al Ru Farm

Ruth Irving is mad about roses. If you ask her which is her favourite rose, she'll say, 'the one I saw last'.

Ask her which is her favourite flower, however, and she'll tell you that it's the iris. Her acclaimed rose garden, Al Ru Farm, near South Australia's Barossa Valley, is about *all* flowers, insists Ruth. 'I like the architecture of the iris, I love the flowers, and the perfume. Roses are so full on. They're such show-offs. They have the biggest party dress in the room, with the most rope petticoats. The iris is subtle,' she says.

Al Ru Farm, set within a Charolais and Brahman cattle stud, is just 17 years old. When Ruth and her husband, Alan, bought the property in 1982, there were just a few ash (*Fraxinus excelsior*) with sheep grazing underneath, close to the stone house. Now the 3-hectare garden is made up of several garden compartments. Each is very different; bursting with vigorous plantings and beautifully designed structures.

Ruth, a dealer in fine eighteenth and nineteenth century antiques, displays the architect's eye in the strong design elements throughout the garden and the artist's use of sometimes quirky colour.

She moves plants in her garden all year round—particularly when they are out in flower. 'That's when you know what you've got,' she says. She spends time walking around the garden, experimenting with colour and design by picking a flower or a leaf and holding it next to different plants. Bronze fennel is teamed, therefore, with the fluffy, burgundy flower heads of the smoke bush (*Cotinus coggygria* 'Velvet Cloak') and backed with a purple-leaved prunus. The cerise-to-chocolate-coloured day lily 'Scarlet Orbit' looks marvellous with this combination.

Close by is an extraordinary arbour of *Wisteria floribunda* 'Macrobotrys', the blue of the long, scented racemes intensified by the cream tea rose 'Devoniensis', and a wonderful sight in early November. Ruth recommends clipping the wisteria immediately after flowering, and then constantly, to keep it from strangling the roses and to ensure successful flowering. Here, a planting of the *Clematis* 'The President' tones with the blue iris 'Loyal Devotion' and the *Clematis* 'Edouard Desfosse' with deep blue late flowering *Iris* 'Distraction'.

While the bearded iris is perhaps the harbinger of summer, Ruth feels that the most underestimated plant in the garden is the day lily (*Hemerocallis* spp.), which flowers throughout the hottest months of the year. 'Day lilies are marvellous for picking. The stems hold up to a dozen buds, and as each flower dies, it can just be broken off to reveal the next,' she says.

The exuberant garden at Al Ru Farm is a combination of lines and axes, as in the formal rose garden of hybrid teas, as well as informal areas. 'I am perhaps less disciplined than some people and therefore I need a little bit of whimsy in my garden,' says Ruth. 'I like winding paths so that you don't know what's around the corner. That gives an air of enchantment.'

Set at the end of a long, formal lawn, which is bordered by deep beds of grey and blue perennials, and yellow roses, is 'The Garden Pavilion', where lucky guests can stay, looking out into their own garden.

Beneath a Hans Heysen picture of river red gums, covered in a mauve wisteria, 'The Garden Pavilion' is yet another vignette in a complicated garden picture.

Left: Exuberance and an eye for colour has created the successful garden at Al Ru Farm.

Moat's Corner

The gardening world is full of marvellous characters. Jean Duncan, who gardens on Victoria's Mornington Peninsula, is definitely one of them. Like many good gardeners she is also generous, regularly sharing her garden with visitors in aid of the charities she supports.

While the climate of the area is gentle, open expanses of cleared farming land have created wind problems. The Monterey cypress (*Cupressus macrocarpa*) is very much a part of the landscape of the Mornington Peninsula, where mature stands form essential windbreaks. At Moat's Corner, they create a mysterious entrance drive to this large country garden, which is set amidst a working property breeding 'belted Galloway' cattle.

The garden, which Jean has created with her husband over 40 years, is a rambling 2.2 hectares. The various areas are linked by strong architectural features such as pergolas, stone steps and retaining walls, all built in a scale in keeping with the size of the garden.

Spacious lawns are linked by pergolas covered in white, pink and lilac wisterias and roses, including 'Buff Beauty', the vigorous *Rosa gigantea* and the cream and pink 'Pierre de Ronsard'.

While Jean is a plant collector, the lake with its waterlilies, surrounded by the graceful weeping willows and yellow water iris, is a lesson in the importance of discipline in choosing plant material. Just the one iris is used, a yellow *I. pseudacorus*. This is another example of the wisdom of planting many of the one species, rather than a few of each of many different plants. At Moat's Corner, carefully chosen statuary complements the dramatic scene.

Below the lake is a woodland area; old oaks are underplanted with swathes of bulbs.

In the bush house are collections of hostas and ferns. There is also a collection of vireya rhododendron, a category of the genus *Rhododendron* which has been in cultivation for over 150 years, but which has only recently gained popularity. 'I love them for their bells and trumpets in fantastic colours which range from oranges to apricots, pinks and whites,' says Jean.

This garden, which is not without its surprises, is for both the plant collector and the student of design. A pair of bronze jabiru stand guard at the entrance to a small Japanese-style garden of conifers and bamboos.

Further on an impressive double border packed with delphiniums, foxgloves, iris and rare white perennial stock is divided by a 3-metre wide grass path. Each deep border is set off by a large wooden pagoda, a place for sitting to contemplate the black and white 'belted Galloways' grazing peacefully in the lush green paddocks just outside the garden gate.

Below: The garden at Moat's Corner is not without its surprises. It is for both the plant collector and the student of design. Here, the lake is surrounded with the iris *I. pseudacorus*.

History made

A typical Australian country house sight—a wisteria rampaging up a water stand—greets the visitor to this historic house in Sydney's south-west. The property, now known as Gledswood, was first settled in 1810, when a building (which later became the kitchen of the homestead) was built. Further buildings, including the cottage where the convicts were housed at night, were erected later and remain today.

Gledswood homestead was built for James Chisholm with convict labour between 1816 and 1829, and the family and descendants lived there for 120 years. The beautiful woodwork throughout the house is in Australian cedar (*Toona australis*) cut from the property.

Today, the 70-hectare property breeds 'belted Galloway' cattle. The property is also a working colonial farm and winery and, according to owner Theresa Testoni, is 'returning the wine, wool and wheat industries to the Macarthur District, the birthplace of Australia's rural wealth.'

The 2.5 hectares of gardens which surround the homestead were refurbished in 1990 by plantswoman, Mary Davis, and are again looking marvellous.

Along the original carriageway that fed into Camden Valley Way is a Chinese elm that must be 180 years old, underplanted with red clivia. The carriageway retains the original edging of convict-made bricks, complete with convict stamps of love hearts and diamonds.

A marvellous, formal, herb garden is only seven years old, and features edges of these bricks, laid on their side in the original manner. The herb garden is divided into sections by paths of red scoria. A standard of the rose 'Sea Foam' is at each outer corner and in the centre are four standards of 'The Fairy', more usually seen as a groundcover. Many of

the herbs are grown from seed imported from Europe; emphasis is on colour and foliage. There is frilly-leaved mustard, Tuscan cabbage, lemon thyme, golden oregano, bronze fennel, and rue, to ward off evil spirits. Pyrethrum daisies and garlic are added as companion planting, and *Chrysanthemum paledosum* has been allowed to self-seed.

Along one side, a mass of cornflowers and French lavender, backed with *Echium fastuosum* turns into a river of blue in high summer. The herb garden is at its peak when roses are out in late October. The roof-line of the arbours which lead the visitor from the herb garden were copied from the original stable roof.

To the eastern side of the house is the formal rose garden which is also planted with perennials such as *Delphinium* 'Pacific Giant' as well as the hard-working penstemons. By large bay windows are beds of massed red tulips, a great sight in July, and of red roses—the fragrant 'Dublin Bay', bred from 'Altissimo', as well as 'Seduction', flowering in September. In this bed, the scented *Heliotropium arborescens* 'Lord Roberts', with its black leaves and purple flowers, looks extraordinary with the wisteria which is in full flower in the last week in September. Again, the original convict bricks have been used to edge the garden beds, making maintenance easier.

On the western side of the house is a charming white garden, containing an original planting of angel's trumpet, *Datura* (now called *Brugmansia*) as well as white cosmos, white honesty and the rose 'Green Ice', one of the best white miniatures. *Lamium maculatum* 'White Nancy', with its silvery leaves, is used as edging and the planting is backed with Manchurian pears, buddlejas, grey cardoons and gardenias.

The new woodland garden will house azaleas and camellias when the canopy cover is established. In the meantime, this area is planted out with marguerite daisies, including the new 'Summer Angel' and

'Summer Melody', which are being trialled for Sydney University.

The various areas of the garden are separated by immaculate kikuyu lawns, which are kept green and lush by oversowing each May with rye grass seed. The kikuyu browns off in the winter temperatures, which drop to −6°C. The rye is lush through spring, but dies off when the December heat hits, leaving the kikuyu to come into its own. The only problem is that it needs weekly mowing. 'But,' say the owners, 'it's worth it!'

Opposite: Built between 1816 and 1829, Gledswood is one of Australia's oldest homes.

Above: The water tank—typical of old homestead gardens.

Bottom left: The herb garden.

How this garden works

* At Gledswood, lawn clippings, garden cuttings and manure are turned into compost in just three weeks and returned to the garden as an essential, water-saving mulch.

* Turn compost bins into a work of art by screening with lattice and covering with roses. At Gledswood they use the clear red 'Altissimo', the repeat-flowering 'Gold Bunny' and the clotted-cream, remontant 'Devoniensis'.

Sounds of Summer

The thwack of the cricket ball against the willow, the uncontrollable laughter of children, the drum of the cicadas and the thick shimmering haze of heat that hangs heavy in the air—these are the comfortable sounds and sights of summer.

There are also the unmistakable summer colours, most particularly that unique blue of the agapanthus that seems so very Sydney, where it flowers while the lazy, endless days of January are still to arrive. In country areas the agapanthus bravely endures the merciless February heat, blooming a bright welcome at front gates when most else is simply gasping to be cut back and readied for winter.

The agapanthus comes from South Africa, collected by such travellers as Georgiana Molloy who stopped at Cape Town in December 1829. Molloy wrote that she spent £7 17s 6d on seeds and she often referred to the joy her plants from the Cape provided around her isolated home set in the rugged country south of Perth.

A garden thug to many and even outlawed by some councils, the agapanthus is a blue of such a particular clarity that it surely deserves a place in the summer garden. The adage 'a weed is just a plant in the wrong place' comes to mind; indeed, what is a weed to one is a treasure to another. Some readers may recall the visit, a few years ago, of a doyenne of the English garden-writing world, in Australia to lecture on treasures for the perennial border. 'Always have a few rare and special plants in your border,' she advised on the first day of her lecture tour, as a shot of an 'aggie' illuminated the projector screen. The room sat politely silent. She ruefully told another writer that it took her just until day two of her tour to realise that the agapanthus is anything but a rare and fragile beauty in this country.

Even at summer's height, when school is back and computers are humming again, there is a sense that the season is on the turn. Another African beauty, the climber, *Stephanotis floribunda*, is blooming, with its waxy cream flowers offering a delicate scent if you pause by her side just long enough.

Above: A summer blaze of agapanthus.

A garden for the birds

The mountain ranges behind the capital cities of Australia are loved by gardeners as the site of 'hill-station' style gardens of cool climate treasures, emulating the grand estates of England. In these wonderful gardens, many of which are over 100 years old, deciduous trees, banks of massive rhododendron and alpine delicacies thrive in the mists and rich soils. The Dandenongs, an hour's drive from the centre of Melbourne, are no exception.

The area is also the site of several beautifully designed gardens of Australian native plants. If your attitude to native gardens is tainted by their misuse in the 1970s, these gardens will turn you into a believer. One such garden is that of Shirley Carn. Shirley's steeply sloping, 1-hectare garden has been terraced for ease of access. Attention to drainage is crucial for Australian natives and beds are built up to ensure that drainage is perfect.

According to Shirley, 'the trick with growing natives is to have a good pair of secateurs and be brutal in cutting back, from the beginning. Colour and form in your planting are most important. Getting the combinations and achieving the groundcover is what takes the time.'

Shirley loves white, blue and yellow plants together. The lemon ironwood (*Backhousia citriodora*) with its lemon-scented leaves and clusters of small white flowers is planted 'for the soul' and underneath, a massed groundcover is achieved with paper daisies. On a top terrace, blue *Scaevola* grows through a pink *Thryptomene*. Nearby, the native wisteria,

Hardenbergia comptoniana, deep blue-purple with a white eye, grows through an apricot *Grevillea*. Next to this vignette is a white *Hardenbergia*.

Elsewhere, a cream form of the climber *Hibbertia denudata* is used as a groundcover. Shirley also loves the *Cistus* genus, which go well with Australian natives. There is *Cistus* 'Silver Pink', a pale pink cultivar with soft, grey-green leaves, with which a deep pink *Helianthemum*, the rock rose, has made itself at home. On a more inaccessible terrace, toward the bottom of the steep slope, are plants which require very little water. Here is an exquisite combination of *Leucophyta brownii* with *Banksia meisneri*.

Surprise is an important element in this garden. Constant little treasures are discovered, so that a walk through the garden is a trip of discovery. Walk around the corner and you'll find treats such as *Darwinia macrostegia* and *D. meeboldii*. Grasses are left for the butterflies; the finches like the seed heads.

'To grow natives you must know their natural habitat,' says Shirley. '*Darwinia* is from around the Stirling Ranges. *Lechenaultia* needs dry conditions, as it's from Western Australia. *Dryandra*, also from Western Australia and planted for the birds, hates wet feet.'

Above: The exquisite and rare white waratah.

Left: Constant little treasures are discovered when you walk though Shirley Carn's garden.

Lush tapestry

Pat and Judy Bowley now garden at Wildes Meadow in the Southern Highlands of New South Wales. Wildes Meadow was named for Joseph Wild (1773–1847), an ex-convict who explored much of the area south to the Monaro Plains. The 12-hectare property is surrounded by hills, milk-coloured in the gentle light.

The entrance to the Bowleys' last garden, at Tumut, was famous for its colour combination of purple-leaved prunus and golden elm. At Wildes Meadow the mix of magentas, bronzes and golds again welcomes the visitor. The long entrance winds past plantings of the smoke bush, *Cotinus coggygria* 'Royal Purple', of golden gleditzia, the purple-leaved hazelnut and gold catalpa. Many sheep graze decoratively

in lush paddocks on either side, and beyond, the rolling hills disappear into the mist that scents the air.

'The garden revolves around trees and water,' says Pat Bowley. Two formal areas, large rectangles, stretch out from the house; a double-sided perennial border is bound by box hedge, and adjoins a formal vegetable garden, protected by a high brick wall, leading to a pleached hornbeam allee. At the limits of the garden are walks that extend into the bog garden and beyond, to the meadow.

In the perennial border is a jigsaw of leaf shapes and textures. There are the greys of stachys, silene, and lychnis, along with *Sedum* 'Vera Jamison', the architectural cardoon and *Paeonia ludlowii*. 'It has never flowered for me,' says Pat. 'And I must have had it for 15 years. The thing must be giddy as it's been in so many different positions. I was very pleased to read that Beth Chatto said she considered it to be a foliage plant because it had never flowered for her either.'

A pink ceanothus flowers constantly along with the violet-flowered *Linaria purpurea* and the so-smart bronze-leaved cow parsley *Anthriscus* 'Ravenswing'. A dozen Irish yews throughout the border tie the plantings together. The beautiful copper-glazed urn by the Bowleys' son Simon rests comfortably in the arrangement.

The eye is drawn to the border opposite by a vigorous *Clematis montana* 'Snowflake', a shower of white in spring. This border is resplendant with *Weigela*, with *Buddleja* and with roses. The deep red Bourbon rose 'Mme Isaac Pereire' leans over the red-leaved *Hebe* x *andersonii* while the greys and blues of catmint weave through.

The border finishes with a sunken garden. Here, pillars support chains swathed in roses and clematis; there is the iceberg rose along with 'Mme Gregoire Staechlin' and 'American Pillar', with *Clematis cirrhosa* var. *balearica*, and the discreet, cream-green flowers of the *Clematis montana* 'Marjorie'.

The vegetable garden is an ellipse, placed within the rectangle and cut into sections. Beds are raised with brick edging. Along the wall is a waist-high bed, half filled with coarse gravel, to tend and display alpine treasures. Artichokes grow down the centre, flanked by large-leaved vegetables and asparagus. In each corner are multi-grafted fruit trees; there are several cultivars of apricot, plum, apple and pear. The reverse of the wall supports thornless blackberry and other espaliered fruit trees.

Below the formal area is a large pond surrounded with prostrate silver willows (*Salix repens* var. *argentea*). *Iris sibirica* of a beautiful deep violet blue is planted around the banks, where the bright pink *Rosa wilmottii* rambles happily.

In the bog garden, the water elder, *Viburnum opulus*, thrives, along with copses of *Betula nigra*, the black birch. The swamp cypress, *Taxodium distichum*, turns an impressive red in autumn. *Gunnera manicata* becomes a giant in summer, and a mass of buttercups flower yellow.

Opposite: At Wildes Meadow, the mix of magentas, bronzes and golds welcomes the visitor.

Left: An urn by potter Simon Bowley, amid the lush tapestry of green.

How this garden works

* In this magnificent garden, heath provides a coathanger for the pink-striped *Clematis* 'Nelly Moser'. Clematis can be propagated mid to end November, from a length including one node, taken from the fresh growth.

* Trees newly planted in the bog garden are stabilised with netting pegged over the well-mulched roots. 'Otherwise, when it rains, and the water comes racing down, I would lose them,' says Pat.

* The fruit trees are protected by a cage constructed from galvanised piping with Downie fittings which join together like a Meccano set, covered with galvanised netting. 'It took a couple of days, with the help of a strong son,' he says.

* Pat cuts his *Buddleja salviifolia* down to the ground after it flowers in early spring.

A contained garden

Moving your horticultural treasures from a large garden to a tiny townhouse plot must be rather like fitting the possessions of a lifetime into an apartment after the children have left home.

Lois Harvey was faced with this challenge when she transferred a quarter-acre garden into a garden on a small concrete slab on the side of her Central Coast 'villa'. She now keeps her treasures in pots and believes you don't have to own an acreage to boast a garden of collectables.

Her plants, including her collection of sought-after clivias, are housed happily in pots. According to Lois, success in container gardening depends upon creating the appropriate environment for each plant. Walls and lattice can be used to create the microclimates they need.

Another key to successful gardening in pots, says Lois, rests in reducing overall scale. 'The small flower is better in a small area than the larger flower. In tiny gardens you are looking also for scent.'

Lois loves the maples (*Acer palmatum* var. *dissectum*), which grow particularly well in a pot. 'You get a lot for your money,' she says. 'You get form and colour. The most wonderful thing with maples is that you see the four seasons of the year. One morning I can look out of the window and see that the leaves are turning. Then I will look out and say. 'Oh, the leaves are falling'. There is always an indication of the season to come.'

Lois continuously experiments with different types of potting mix. 'When I buy a plant, I ask the grower what he is using. I now have a collection of all different types of potting mix to which I add rice hulls and peanut shells—anything I can get my hands on. Most plants have to be potted on each year, into a pot one size larger,' she advises. She

doesn't use water crystals as she finds they hold too much water, adversely affecting drainage.

Lois belongs to several societies which reflect her interest in clivias, orchids, camellias and begonias. 'Clivias like their roots restricted and undisturbed,' she says. 'They are a wonderful plant for around trees. They don't need fertiliser, although a folar fertiliser is helpful. They don't need much water; in fact, they'll rot if they get too wet. Clivias need good drainage—a scoria mixture is perfect. They do need shelter in frost areas—grow them under awnings. They don't like morning sun, but don't seem to mind hot afternoon sun. They love being in pots and need the root system to be cramped to flower and to make "pups".'

Lois has bred the covetted cream clivia and has crossed the cream with the usual orange to create a peach-coloured flower. In the young plants, the cream-flowered clivia has a green base, while the orange-flowered clivia are red at the base of the young leaves.

Orchids do marvellously in the microclimate in this tiny garden. To those of us who have come to the conclusion that the only way to have orchids in flower is to buy them each year, Lois says that morning sun is absolutely essential.

Camellias also earn their keep in a small space. The species, often scented, and the miniature japonicas, are particularly hard working. A dark corner of a courtyard might be lit by the variegated *Camellia japonica* 'Benten' or *C. j.* 'Autumn Glory'.

Camellia sasanqua lends itself to hedging, and clipping, while the *japonica* 'Nuccio's Gem'—surely the most perfect of all camellias—is ideal for training along horizontal wires to cover a wooden side-fence or dividing wall.

If you are particularly lucky, you might find the tiny pink miniature *Camellia japonica* 'Rosiflora Cascade', perfectly suited for growing in a pot or small space.

Opposite left: The luscious fruit of the clivia provide glamour for months.

Opposite right: Lois Harvey's clivias thrive happily in pots.

Above: Another favourite found in this garden is the maple *Acer palmatum* var. *dissectum*.

How this garden works

* Think of the scale of your garden, which will be more successful if the leaves and flowers correspond in size.

* Clivias enjoy being pot bound, hate being water-logged and need frost protection.

* Creating the appropriate environment for your plants is essential. Study how they grow in the wild to prevent heartbreak.

Moving north

It's virtually impossible to do justice to Lindy and Hamish Dalziell's Queensland garden, in either words or pictures. Located at Buderim, in the hinterland behind the Sunshine Coast, the garden seems to hang from the mountainside, affording views of some 250°, east to the Pacific Ocean and north across the Maroochy River and the canefields to Mount Cooroy, and Mount Ninderry.

The house, which is set low into the 2-hectare property, opens onto a wide grass terrace and swimming pool. Those spectacular mountains in the near distance are very much part of the garden picture. To the left of the arrangement is a trumpet tree (*Tabebuia* spp.) splashing the sky with canary yellow in spring. 'It's only in flower for one month a year, but worth

it,' says Lindy Dalziell. Close by, the spreading canopy of the poinciana (*Delonix regia*) provides wonderful shade without imposing upon the view.

A duranta hedge, inset with huge pots, backs the pool. (Also in the garden is another hedge of duranta, of the cultivar 'Sheena's Gold'; the new leaves are lime green, the older foliage darker green, turning gold in very hot weather.)

To the west of the house is a favourite part of the garden, a rainforest gully through which a stream runs after rain. This area has been restored and re-created over the 10 years that the Dalziells have owned the property; heliconias and cordylines now thrive in the cool shade, and welcome protection from the sun is provided for the house. Soft-cane dendrobiums cling to the trees, living on air and flowering year after year. Bromeliads love the dappled light; there is *Neoregelia* 'Fireball' and *N.* 'Foster's Little Gem' as well as Spanish moss, (*Tillandsia usneoides*), also a bromeliad.

Hamish Dalziell has gardening in his blood; his great great grandfather was Joseph Henry Maiden, second Director of Sydney's Botanic Gardens which had been founded in 1816 by Governor Macquarie. He is reclaiming from camphor laurel an area of rainforest at the base of the garden. 'It will probably be long term,' says his wife. 'I look at this area and feel faint, but Hamish has unbelievable patience. We adjoin the Buderim rainforest park, so we have lovely rainforest trees and wonderful birdlife.'

To the rear of the house are sweeping lawns bound by long flower borders. Here, Louisiana iris do well, along with day lilies and watsonias. In the midst of the lawn is a candlenut tree (*Aleurites moluccana*), native to Queensland. The nut, according to J. H. Maiden in his *Useful Native Plants of Australia*, published in 1889, 'is similar in flavour to the common walnut, and very wholesome. It is, however, rather rich, from the quantity of oil it contains.'

Underneath, birds nest ferns thrive on the humus and debris from above. Another special tree in this park-like area is the tipu (*Tipuana tipu*), a South American shade tree. There is the tung-oil tree (*Vernicia fordii*), from southern China, showing off its cream trumpet flowers for the first time, after five years.

A new area, for quiet sitting, is inspired by the gardens of Japan. Here, a pepper tree, *Schinus areira*, shades a dwarf, clumping bamboo. Great care was taken when lighting the garden. 'Less is more' is particularly important when it comes to lighting, says Lindy. 'The most magical is in this Japanese garden,' she says. 'It's very soft, both up-lighting and down.'

The candlenut tree is highlighted with up-lighting, as are the 30-metre high hoop pines and the Cuban royal palm (*Roystonea regia*) which provides a focal point to the end of the long driveway.

Gardening in the tropics provides its own special challenges, of course. 'The difficult thing about gardening in this climate is there is no time when you can close the garden down,' says Lindy. And, perhaps like gardeners everywhere, she admits to a passion for what she just can't have.

Opposite: Bromeliads thrive in the dappled light.

Above: A quiet corner.

Bottom left: Soft-stem dendrobiums are happy to live on air.

How this garden works

* *Duranta* spp. forms a fast growing hedge. It needs to be clipped from time of planting; monthly in summer.

* In the rainforest area in Hamish and Lindy Dalziell's garden, invasive bamboo has been eliminated by cutting and painting with a glyphosate-based poison.

* Soft leaved buffalo, carpet grass and 'Durban' are grasses that do well in humid climates.

Autumn

By a lazy river

As you might imagine from the name, it's not only the garden that entices at Lunch on the Pond. Once you have wandered through the old garden, part of the Lower St Vigeans Estate, at Stirling in the Adelaide Hills, you can relax on the wide deck reaching over the peaceful lily pond, to enjoy owner Judith Quigley's home cooking.

An enchanting woodland garden—the sort of place where children can create their own magic—Judith's garden is part of the heritage of the Hills. The entire garden was planted after Professor Edward Stirling, later Sir Edward, politician, surgeon, scientist, explorer and avid plant collector, built his magnificent house in 1880. Judith's section of the estate boasts many heritage trees from that time.

'In autumn the copper beeches are to die for,' says Judith. 'They're some of the biggest trees in the garden, and are all from the earliest days.' Brilliant autumn yellows are provided by the huge leaves of the chestnut oak, which dates from the 1880s.

A massive bull bay magnolia, planted in 1881, and which must be more than 30 metres across its dome, covers the garden in scent throughout December, January and February. Magnificent Douglas firs border the lawn areas. Perhaps Judith's favourite tree is an English oak, more than 100 years old, that shades the 1880s gardener's shed. 'The shed still has its original pine flooring and a little oak seat. Recently an old lady came up to me in the garden and asked to see where her father used to sit. It turned out her father was Mr Wibbley, the first gardener.'

The most visited tree in the garden must be the Californian redwood, *Sequoia sempervirens*, which is heritage listed. 'The number of people who hug that tree,' says Judith. 'People who are into trees say it gives out energy. When I have been sad, I have gone out and hugged it every night.'

From the end of September the mollis azaleas put on a brilliant show of scented, orange and yellow blooms. 'Underneath the mollis is the most wonderful patch of very old lily-of-the-valley, both pink and cream. The perfume is heavenly.'

After the mollis azaleas the rhododendron continue the parade. There is the heavily scented *Rhododendron* 'Fragrantissimum' as well as the old favourite, the hybrid *R.* 'Pink Pearl', now over 7 metres high. *R.* 'Mrs E. C. Stirling', named after Sir Edward Stirling's wife, has a pale pink flower and was planted over 100 years ago.

The Adelaide Botanic Gardens has recognised the importance of some of the plants in this old garden. Among the shrubs is a rare burgundy flowered variety of weigela that the Gardens' experts have named 'Eva Rathke'.

Secret paths take the explorer along either side of the pond, through stands of clumping bamboo as old as the garden.

The wisterias at Lunch on the Pond are spectacular in early October, with a white wisteria towering over the pond. However, peak time in the garden is perhaps in mid November, when over 150 old fashioned roses are a mass of creams and pinks. Judith's favourite rose is the too-temperamental 'Souvenir de la Malmaison', which, in this setting, at last behaves like the lady she is.

While this is a garden for daily enjoyment, if Judith Quigley were forced to choose a favourite time it would be spring 'because it's the beginning of three beautiful seasons—and the blackbirds sing'.

Opposite: Lunch is served on the verandah by the lake.

Bottom left: The early autumn colours of *Parrotia persica*.

Below: A tranquil moment.

How this garden works

* The *Pittosporum* 'James Stirling', makes an extremely effective hedge in this garden.

* The weigelas in the garden are cut back cane by cane from the base of the plant, after flowering in spring.

Halls of splendour

Nowhere is the bold design gesture seen better than at Parliament House in our national capital. Nowhere is the use of grand sweeps of plant material more effective. On the approach to the entrance at Parliament House are 1.2 hectares of the groundcover conifer (*Juniperus sabina*), a brave, but successful, planting.

When Parliament House first opened, the visitor could have been forgiven for feeling that it was all too much. Too big, too brash, and—is one allowed to say this about the seat of our nation?—too vulgar.

Ten years later, however, it has settled into its site and the surrounding landscaping. The concrete-mix walls have mellowed but not muddied, the beautiful marbles of the interiors have softened, and the exquisite marquetry of Australian flora by artist Michael Retter is bright and breathtaking. The building is awe-inspiring, and now looks appropriately magnificent as the place of government.

The extensive gardens were designed as a setting of appropriate scale and spirit for the building. The entire site is 33 hectares with the building and hard surfaces covering 10 hectares. Twenty-three hectares are landscaped using various themes—there are large areas of brilliant green turf (a particular challenge with the strange weather Canberra can experience); there are impressive plantings of native species outside the buildings, formal flower gardens, and the Parliamentarians' courtyard gardens.

These 17 private courtyards are set between the buildings, and were designed to be simple, functional and restful, for quiet contemplation. These are small areas of inspired restraint and formality, to be enjoyed by walking through them, or by viewing them from the building. You could forgive a politician for not wanting to return to the scrum of question time.

Left: The various gardens and courtyards of Australia's Parliament House were designed to promote quiet contemplation.

How this garden works

* The sedums 'Autumn Joy' and 'Ruby Glow' make successful bold plantings, providing interest in the border into autumn. They clump up well for easy division in winter. Try them, in swathes, backed by massed Japanese blood grass (*Imperata cylindrica* 'Rubra', and the so-smart golden grasses, *Calamagrostis* x *acutiflora* 'Karl Foerster'.

* To help you remember the pruning decisions you made when a tree was in leaf, tie a piece of wool on any dead or crossing branches to prune later, in winter.

Anlaby

Garden writers are constantly meeting people who are pretty extraordinary—people who inspire you to do better, to try harder, and who seem to keep a steady eye on a very big picture. It can be somewhat daunting to see the prodigious talent of others and the courage with which they take on constant challenges, but mostly it's completely uplifting, and it's always an enormous privilege.

The owners of Anlaby station, Hans and Gill Albers, are such people. The Albers are only the third family to own this significant property in its 150-year history and now the gardens have been opened so that the public can appreciate our pastoral, horticultural and literary history.

Anlaby was established in 1839, when a run of 48.6 hectares near Kapunda, in South Australia, was taken up by Frederick Hansborough Dutton. Eighteen thousand sheep were bought from New South Wales and the run was gradually extended to 28 350 hectares. Anlaby became world famous for its Merino wool with 30 men shearing 60 000 sheep.

The property perhaps reached its height under Henry Dutton who inherited Anlaby in 1890. The house was extended to the grand Victorian homestead that it is today, and the Italianate façade, descending by a flight of stone steps to a generous grass terrace, was added. The gardens were extended to 16 hectares and became world-renowned. Fourteen gardeners, some brought from England, were employed to maintain the terraces, lawns, flower gardens and parkland. Conservatories were built for camellias, orchids and vegetables; there were lily ponds and more than 6000 roses in several rose gardens.

In 1905 Dutton's son Henry Hampden Dutton married Emily Martin; the iron fountain set in the main grass terrace was made in her family's foundry. She was a passionate gardener, a noted concert pianist, violinist and an artist. After her husband's death in 1932 Emily ran the property, by then 3240 hectares, and added the library. Her son, the writer Geoffrey Dutton, was born at Anlaby in 1922; his writing tower, the Folly Water Tower, still stands at the bottom of the garden.

Hans and Gill Albers are gradually restoring the gardens, now of 1 hectare. Parrots, peacocks and possums are among the many challenges. 'The peacocks eat everything under their noses, the possums eat the rosebuds and then the parrots come and finish the job.'

Many important trees remain, including a bunya pine, bur oaks, a peppercorn *circa* 1850 and five enormous Chinese elms from 1900—but a program of tree surgery is desperately needed. The wonderful 2-kilometre planting of sugar gums along the drive is over 100 years old.

Throughout the gardens, collections of original roses remain, many identified by rosarian Walter Duncan. In the wild garden is a single white Banksian rose, as well as *R.* 'Trigintipetala', the ancient Damask used for the production of 'attar of roses'. In the lower rosary, dating to the last century, is a hedge of the *spinossissima* rose, with its single flowers and black hips.

There is a collection of roses by the Australian breeder Alister Clark, including 'Squatter's Dream' which grows over the balustrade to the house. His 'Sunny South' and 'Black Boy' climb the 1880s rose arches, along with 'American Pillar', the massive Cherokee rose, and 'Mermaid', probably planted by Emily. 'Every time I go to do something a bit too grand, I feel Emily telling me not to, telling me that you can't work against this harsh climate,' says Gill. 'Emily is very much here. You just know that she has tried so hard to save the garden.'

Below: Anlaby Station and the homestead.

Cloudehill

After desperately-needed early autumn rain in 1998, and somewhat cooler days, Victoria's mountain gardens were looking marvellous. Cool-climate trees such as the tulepo (*Nyassa sylvatica*), the ash (*Fraxinus* spp.) and the beech (*Fagus* spp.) were putting on a tapestry of reds, pinks, yellows and golds to illuminate the mellow harvest months.

One garden not to be missed in autumn—or indeed in any season of the year—is Cloudehill in the Dandenongs, just behind Melbourne. It's a garden of grand ambition, and of huge success—and it's also a garden where one can learn a great deal.

The 2.2-hectare garden has existed since 1990, when owners Jeremy Francis and Valerie Campbell-Wemyss came to the Dandenongs from Western Australia, dreaming of soft vistas and flamboyant borders of the rare and tender plants they had loved in the United Kingdom.

The garden is created as a series of terraces, each home to wonderful cool-climate trees, now a blaze of autumn colour. Several trees, including mature copper beech, were imported from England in 1928. There is a also massive *Magnolia denudata*, as well as two weeping maples (*Acer palmatum* 'Dissectum Atropurpureum'), shipped from Japan by the Yokohama trading company in the 1920s, and perhaps the finest in Australia.

Several axes display the work of some of Australia's finest artists. Ted Seacombe's glorious plum-glaze porcelain pot contains the prostrate

Abies amabilis 'Spreading Star'. A little further on, a large urn in a delicate apple-green glaze is offset by a *Rhododendron schlippenbachii*, also brought to Australia in the 1920s. In autumn, this rhododendron turns scarlet, and in spring, bears soft pink, perfumed flowers on bare stems. Nearby is the very weeping *Acer palmatum* 'Waterfall', a new variety.

The bones of this garden have been created by hedges of hornbeam, beech, rhododendron and cedar (*Thuja* spp.). A favourite plant for hedging is the hornbeam (*Carpinus betulus*), a classic hedging plant in the Northern Hemisphere. 'It gives the impression of beech but is much easier,' says Jeremy. Another favourite is the new *Thuja occidentalis* 'Smaragd', an intense emerald-green in mid summer, turning to bronze in winter. 'It's slow growing, which is essential for detail and finish,' he adds.

The herbaceous borders at Cloudehill are justly famous, and were among the first to display such show-ponies as *Crocosmia* 'Lucifer' and the chocolate cosmos (*Cosmos atrosanguineus*). The complicated borders are divided into three main flowering periods: in the early part of the summer season, delphiniums and penstemons provide drama; in the mid season, the bergamots (*Monarda* spp.)—much underestimated—get to work.

The *Dahlia* 'Bishop of Llandaff', with its smart black foliage, the new *Dahlia* 'Fire Mountain' with double, pure red, flowers and black foliage, and the burnt-orange to yellow flowers of *Dahlia* 'Yellow Hammer', add

colour in the last part of the summer season, along with the sedums, such as 'Autumn Joy'. 'And for each part of the season you must have two or three good doers which will fill in,' says Jeremy. The grasses are used to this effect throughout the summer and carry the garden through autumn to winter. The tough *Miscanthus sinensis* 'Variegata' connects the different sections of a long border, lights up a dark corner, or leads the eye along a certain path. In winter the grasses provide movement and rustle, before they are cut back and divided. New imports at Cloudehill include 'Flamingo', 'Purpurascens' and 'Silver Feather', all cultivars of *Miscanthus sinensis*.

The borders are not all cut back at once. 'The messy things are cut back early in winter,' says Jeremy. 'The rest, such as the grasses, are cut late in winter.'

The meadow area at Cloudehill is a mass of naturalised spring bulbs among fine winter and spring grasses. The meadow is slashed in mid-December and reverts to rough green grass.

On the top terrace a small compartment houses a glass and water sculpture by Rudi Jass. Jeremy believes you must be careful about using too much sculpture—one beautiful piece is enough. 'The use of sculpture needs more thought than anything else you do in your garden,' he says.

Opposite: Bold plantings and colourful structures are found at Cloudehill.

Above: Beautiful pieces by some of Australia's finest artists are displayed in the garden.

Left: Gardening on a grand scale.

Wombat Park

Among the many delights of membership of the Australian Garden History Society (AGHS) are the marvellous tours arranged to old and precious country gardens. It's an added thrill to find that some of those gardens are emerging from major, and most successful, renovation.

Just 112 kilometres from Melbourne, and close to the 'goldfields' towns of Castlemaine, Daylesford and Hepburn Springs, is 140-year-old Wombat Park. The original part of this 2.5-hectare garden dates from 1857, created by the Rt Hon William Edward Stanbridge, after he bought a section of a well-known squatting lease, in 1851.

The 'old garden' developed by Stanbridge is now a 1 hectare arboretum of some 250 mature trees. A dense forest, carpeted in autumn with leaves of many colours, shades an original summer house and bird aviary; thousands of bulbs have naturalised throughout. In the pale light of mid May, with the golds of generous, solid trees lighting up the swirling mists and welcome rain, and sheep grazing as if placed by 'Capability' Brown, you could be in the picturesque setting of an eighteenth century English landscape. (It seems likely that the arborist Baron Ferdinand Von Mueller, the first director of the Royal Botanic Gardens, in Melbourne, who was creating the Botanic garden at Daylesford at the same time, would have been a visitor to Wombat Park.)

Extensions, now known as the 'new garden', were commissioned in 1910 by Stanbridge's daughter, Mrs Herbert Cox, and laid out by Gavin Fleming from the Mount Macedon firm of nurserymen, Taylor and Sangster. The new garden, set around the homestead, is a family garden of terraced flower beds leading out to the surrounding grazing land—views captured by the landscape painter, Eugene von Guerard. Perhaps

the most striking feature of this section of the garden is a 90-year-old, 4-metre high, tapestry hedge of variegated holly, golden holly, pittosporums, laurels and the Irish strawberry tree, set around the carriage circle.

Bordering the croquet lawn, to the south of the house, is a crenellated hedge, clipped, in blocks, into different heights. Its dense green sets off perfectly the brilliant autumn cerise of a rare *Enkianthus perulatus*. The croquet lawn is bordered by massive trees which, along with the entrance avenue of 100 mature English elms, are on the National Trust Significant Tree Register.

Head gardener Stewart Henderson (and the total gardening team, except for the crucial weekends when the AGHS lend many hands in a 'working bee'), has been at the Wombat Park garden for 12 years, first working for William Stanbridge's great grand-daughter, Mrs Florence Brooke. 'Mrs Brooke was in her late 80s when she decided to overhaul the old garden, realising its significance,' recalls Henderson. 'She was the only person who knew what was where.'

Standing in the cathedral-like centre of a multi-trunked cypress, which has suckered into dozens of delicate columns, Henderson says, 'The joy of this garden is pretty overwhelming. I have a great relationship with big trees. I'm very involved in the history and the feel of the place.'

Soft paths of fallen leaves and pine needles have formed between the trees, and are lined with hedges of old box. 'Care of the hedges is a critical part of the garden,' says Henderson. 'They must be cut, religiously, each year.' Maintenance of the important trees is also crucial. 'We have a regular program of removing old and dead wood as it appears,' he adds. Among the many trees he loves, the towering Douglas fir (*Pseudotsuga menziesii*) is perhaps his favourite tree. 'Mrs Brooke loved that tree. She allowed the branches to sweep the ground—she loved the natural shape.'

Few will agree when the new owners claim they have, so far, contributed very little. 'There is so much we would like to do, but there are things that must be done first,' they say. 'There are so many rare plants here that are reaching their senescence. They must be replaced somewhere—perhaps as specimen trees in the park.'

Wombat Park is indeed fortunate to have inherited new custodians who understand its place in Australia's pastoral and garden history.

Opposite: Autumn is spectacular in the 140-year-old landscape garden at Wombat Park.

Above: A striking feature of this garden is the 90-year-old, 4-metre-high tapestry hedge of variegated holly, golden holly, pittosporums, laurels and the Irish strawberry tree.

Sea change

Sited within the sea scent of the place the locals call 'the back beach', on Victoria's Mornington Peninsula, are two gardens that don't impose upon the indigenous bushland but, rather, are part of the integrity of the surrounding environment.

Fiona Brockhoff is a landscape designer who, with Jane Burke, a botanist specialising in coastal revegetation, and two other partners, creates restful gardens that don't battle the elements.

The visitor to their adjoining gardens gets a sense that they are completely at home with the landscape within which they are working. Burke's gravel garden is planted with stipas, with the local grass *Poa poiformis* var. *ramifer*, and the cushionbush (*Leucophyta brownii*). The

cushionbush has specific needs—good ventilation, humidity and salt—that are met in this site.

So how can the lay person, wherever he lives, acquire the knowledge to create an environmentally appropriate garden? Jane Burke advises contacting Greening Australia. 'They'll have lists of indigenous growers—but also, keep your eyes open. If you see something that grows beautifully around where you live, get a piece of it and show it to the nursery. He'll say "Oh you live there, do you. I have just the provenance for you". And buy in tube size because the plants don't transplant easily.'

The designers' approach is practical. 'People can be critical if you are not totally indigenous,' says Brockhoff. 'But we use many of the West

Australian plants.' She loves the native hibiscus, *Alyogyne huegelii*. 'It grows by the saltwater streams in W.A. so it's salt tolerant. It has a different leaf colour and tone, which is useful, and a lilac flower. You have to look at plants from a design sense and select them for their form and leaf colour.' Brockhoff designs with the environment rather than against it. 'It doesn't make a lot of sense to me to truck out all your soil, bring in new, foreign soil with a different set of weeds, plant iceberg roses and box hedges and pour on the water and the money. Better to work with what you've got and select appropriate plants.'

When looking at a new site Brockhoff firstly walks around the area to see what's growing well. 'Look at what's there ... and remove coastal weeds to discover the remnant vegetation.' Her design will depend on the client, ' ... if it's a weekender, if they're elderly, if they have children, on the style of the house—but most of these plants can be used formally or informally'.

The sea box, *Alyxia buxifolia* is a favourite plant. 'It's like English box, but more handsome. It hasn't been used extensively and we are still trialling it.' Brockhoff maintains that there are alternatives to hedging. 'You can use brush fencing. Or combinations of shrubs and trees will give an informal boundary that may be more relevant to the house.'

In Brockhoff's garden, the view is crucial; she wouldn't plant red geraniums, which would distract the eye. '*Imposing* your design is the

wrong word,' she says. 'It's about marrying the elements, working with what's here. And it's a huge relief to know you don't have to go out and mow the lawns every week. If I am putting energy into the garden it is into the productive areas, the orchard or the vegie garden.'

Opposite: A thong tree shows life is not always serious in Fiona Brockhoff's garden.

Top: *Isolepsis nodosa* and the grey-foliaged *Cotyledon undulata*.

Above: Jane Burke's gravel garden, which plays host to the *Hebe* 'Autumn Glory'.

Left: An alternative to English Box, *Alyxia buxifolia*.

No huffing and puffing

When you look at the house that Shelley Cullen has built you begin to understand what she means by 'sculpting your environment'. Shelley has built a straw bale studio on what must be one of the most breathtaking sites in the world.

Shelley talks about progress with modification. She uses the word 'visitor', rather than 'tourist', to describe the people who fall in love with all that the area offers. You sense that everything she does is with respect for the environment she has inherited but which she has not taken for granted—and you get the feeling that she is not alone.

Shelley also built the stone house in which she lives near her family's winery. 'I love building,' she says. 'My houses are not the greatest works of art but each time you build you feel a deep sense of satisfaction.' The smaller the better, she adds, paraphrasing Leonardo da Vinci: 'A small house strengthens the mind, a large one weakens it.'

Her straw bale studio, blending into its beautiful and pristine environment on the West Australian coast, is so appropriate that it appears to be part of an emerging Margaret River vernacular architecture. 'You have rounded walls; the soft flowing lines are restful. You don't have a straight up and down structure. It feels as if it's part of the sky; a little sky house'

The building is set amid sheets of white arum lilies. The severe winds which buffet the exposed site on this awe-inspiring cliff have provided a natural canvas for the arum lily which has become something of a weed in Western Australia. The pioneers of early last century, who collected South African plants on their journeys from Britain, have been blamed for the dissemination of many of the Cape plants, including freesias and the Cape daisy, which have been all too content in the warm Western Australian climate.

At Shelley Cullen's straw bale house, the bath is set outside, looking across to the amazing cliffs, but protected from the winds by the indigenous hakeas. The fireplace, built into a corner of the 'porch' is protected from the wind by a wall of perspex sandwiched between two sheets of acrylic—also preserving the breathtaking views. 'The idea in Australia of an indoor–outdoor room is very important,' says Cullen.

Pots of clear red pelargoniums offset perfectly the yellow oxide added to the limestone render which covers the straw bales to form the walls. Limestone render also covers the wind barriers of corrugated iron which protect the groves of fruit trees. There are figs and mulberries and Shelley is trialling five cultivars of fruiting olive; all are thriving in the limestone soil, with a thick layer of straw mulch to conserve moisture. The herb garden is also thriving. 'The concentration is on Mediterranean plants, which can be expected to withstand the extremes of temperatures and the winds,' she says.

Power is provided by a solar tracker which follows the sun, and a wind generator. 'It's a great place of solace. It's 100 per cent non toxic; there are no chemicals here. If someone was really sick and they wanted to come to a pure place, they could come here.'

The view alone is enough to fully rejuvenate the body and make the spirits truly soar.

Opposite and above: Shelley Cullen's straw bale studio has withstood the rigours of its wild setting and blends in perfectly with the Margaret River vernacular architecture.
Below: An outdoor bathroom—enough to inspire any body and soul.

The garden that nature intended

The setting for Rhonda and Bill Daly's property, Milgadara, is extraordinary, nestled against the Black Range near the New South Wales town of Young. With the assistance of designer Kath Carr, the Dalys have created a garden of great peace and beauty that is completely at home in its quintessential Australian setting.

Kath Carr was a disciple of the Victorian garden designer Edna Walling. Visiting Walling over a period of 10 years from her home at Binalong, in south-western New South Wales, Carr's work is reminiscent of that of Walling, but certainly not derivative. She, like Walling, admonished against anything that was not as nature would have intended, repeatedly advising, 'bring the landscape into your garden picture' and 'don't gild the lily'.

'Kath would always try to pick up on the plantings on your property,' says Rhonda Daly today. 'If you had silver pears or almonds, she would repeat them.' Carr's notes from her first visit to Milgadara, on 9 March, 1982, state, 'Setting beautiful—natural. Pottery hut—shingles—espalier pear on end. Must have definite connection between hut and house—meaning, connect outbuildings to house. Repetition of plants leading across.'

Perhaps Kath Carr's most important advice to her garden owners was, 'look for vistas'. 'She would tell you what vistas to frame. You would start at the front gate, and drive in as would a visitor,' says Rhonda. 'She would then take you into the house, to decide on your planting, ensuring that you weren't blocking the views from the windows.'

To this end, Carr always removed telephone lines, hid poles with planting and 'painted out' fence posts in the colour of the surrounding landscape. 'She loved "scrub gum green", a Taubmans colour,' says Rhonda. 'And if you had to paint your roof, she would look at what was in the background, and paint the roof a similar colour.'

Like Walling, Kath Carr observed how nature places trees. 'She doesn't place them in straight lines, she puts them in clumps, and doesn't mix the species too much.' Similarly, Carr advised keeping everything simple. Country house signs were just a name burnt into a plank and painted with creosote, ideally attached to a heavy slab fence.

She talked of framing the view with trees on either side of the garden picture, rather than surrounding yourself, or creating a tunnel effect. 'You don't want to be hemmed in,' explains Rhonda. 'And she wanted you to look down onto water.'

Carr advised planting on the garden perimeter whatever was indigenous, thus bringing the landscape into the garden. The deciduous trees would be painted at the front of the garden picture, closer to the house. She loved groupings of crabapples—*Malus* 'Gorgeous', *Malus* x *purpurea* and *M. spectabilis*—not only to give continuous blossom throughout spring, but for their 'ballerina arms'.

Carr's philosophy was to create mystery by bringing the visitor right around the perimeter of the garden, to catch glimpses of the house, before entering the 'garden proper'. The house was always simple, low and unostentatious. 'She said you shouldn't look up to the house,' remembers Rhonda. 'She would lower the house into the background. And she would recommend plants in threes. There would be two here, and then, one, over there. You'd always "throw" one away.'

Kath Carr loved silver pears teamed with the paperbark, *Melaleuca styphelioides*. Another favourite was *Eriocephalus africanus*, the African cotton bush, which Edna Walling called 'the quiet one'. 'She used to plant the Mudgee wattle, *Acacia spectabilis* with almonds,' says Rhonda. 'It had the fine foliage she loved, and the almond provided depth.'

'I believe it was all in her eye,' Rhonda continues. 'She just perceived it. She never wrote about it, she never drew it. She saw it and she knew what had to happen.'

Opposite: Kath Carr's beloved *Sideroxylon rosea*, the mugga ironbark.

Left: Milgadara is nestled against the Black Range near the town of Young, in south-western New South Wales.

How this garden works

* Look out from your windows when planning where trees should be placed. Always use stakes to mark where trees might be planted. Live with those stakes for several weeks, until you're sure the position is right.

* When planting bulbs Kath Carr would pick the shadowline of a tree and plant under the shadows.

* Kath Carr liked to see the tyre tracks of cars up through the natural grass. She liked grass, not lawn, which she said was 'too maintained looking'.

Highland fling

Gabrielle and Stephen Moore's garden, near the northern New South Wales city of Lismore, is seven different gardens in one, all set down 0.5 hectare of steeply sloping mountainside.

While gardening at an angle creates its own design challenges, the magnificent views of this garden, which looks towards the Tweed Border Ranges, have also dictated the choice of plant material. 'We don't plant anything in front of our view,' says Gabrielle. 'And we've chosen plants that won't grow too high.'

The Moores have been creating their garden since the early 1990s; nothing existed when they bought the house and land. Their soil is 'hard clay', according to Gabrielle. Rainfall is not always as high as you might expect in a sub-tropical climate; the garden is heavily mulched, therefore, with aged tea-tree mulch from the local industry.

In one part of the garden, the Moores wanted a rainforest canopy under which rhododendron, camellia and azaleas would thrive in the acid soil. The canopy has been created with the prized Australian red cedar (*Toona ciliata*), the kurrajongs, or brachychitons, including the spectacular flame tree *Brachychiton acerifolius*, and the smaller-growing lacebark kurrajong (*Brachychiton discolor*), with its flaking green, brown and grey bark and its spectacular deep pink bell-shaped flowers.

Another much-loved group of plants, also acid soil loving, are the magnolia and michelia genera. Gabrielle's favourite tree in the garden is a *Magnolia grandiflora*, which fills the air with its sweet lemony scent from spring until early winter. The garden also houses the *Michelia champaca*, which comes from the Himalayas; its fragrant yellow flowers bloom through summer until after Easter.

Another part of the garden has been set aside for grevilleas, planted to attract birds. The whipbird, with its beautiful call like the sound of a whip, finishing with a bell ring, is now the first to be heard in the early mornings, through the mists which cling to the mountainside and hang in the valley below. There are also wrens, doves, and of course, the colourful lorikeets.

The garden houses a marvellous collection of sub-tropical flowering trees, an education for anyone from a more temperate part of the country. There is the ivory curl spotted silky oak, *Buckinghamia celsissima*, a small rainforest tree with prolific cream tubular blooms which fill the garden with a honey scent in autumn, when little else is flowering. There is also the beautiful evergreen South African cape chestnut, *Calodendrum capense*, with its mauve-pink flowers.

The garden is situated in a koala corridor; Gabrielle has planted the lemon scented gum, *Eucalyptus citriodora*, (now known as *Corymbia citriodora*), to provide shelter and food for these charming, if at times noisy, additions to the garden.

Left: The magnificent *Magnolia grandiflora*.

How this garden works

* Gabrielle and Stephen Moore's steeply sloping garden has been terraced for ease of access and maintenance as well as to prevent erosion and to aid water conservation.

* Gabrielle turns composted tea-tree bark into her heavy clay soil with a three pronged pick, to improve the soil structure and to help preserve moisture.

Tropical paradise

If ever there was an example of the homily that nature is the best teacher of all, it is in the beautiful Whitsunday Islands off the central eastern coast of Queensland. The islands plunge, forest-covered, as in the most delicate of china paintings, into waters of the purest azure. Beaches are fringed with sloping palm trees. Far coastlines of mainland or adjacent islands are shrouded, mystical and ethereal, in mist.

In the tropical north, nature has some landscape design lessons. Massed palms have arranged themselves in swathes, bending gracefully toward the sea. In nature's plan, there is not a vertical line to be seen. Anything that's not beautiful—a blue bucket on a beach, a cigarette butt left on white sand, an orange plastic trough in which you are expected to rinse your sandy feet, but which in fact has ended up as a garbage bin—is the work of humans.

Even in paradise, you realise that the buyer had better beware. Those brochures of swimmers snorkling among coral and coloured tropical fish don't explain that, in fact, these holiday essentials can't be found at your resort—you'll need to further outlay many hundreds of dollars to get to the reef to see them. This brings me to the subject of buying anything that might be classed as mechanical. There is surely nothing more frustrating than being sold a piece of equipment by a man who demonstrates how simple it is to use. With the flick of a switch, he vacuums up a few leaves, 'whipper snips' with ease, trims the hedge and mows your lawn. Beware. Once that salesman is gone, reality strikes. You try it. You can't lift it, even if you could get the jolly thing to start. My advice is: girls, buy from a girl, preferably a small one.

To return to the topic, however, many of the tropical plants are scented. Think of the glorious night-scented jessamine (*Cestrum nocturnum*)—divine after dark. It's easy to propagate and makes the most delicious, scented hedge, which can be clipped once the flowers have finished.

Like all plants, tropical varieties can look wonderful if used properly—and that usually means in blocks, rather than dotted about. Even the oft-derided umbrella tree (*Schefflera actinophylla*), which looks tragic standing alone, is terrific in a crowd.

You don't have to feel that you're living in a sauna to create a jungle of heliconias, cannas, begonias and gingers, as all of these plants can boast species which will grow well in cool climates.

Above: The fiery-orange *Canna* x *generalis* adds amazing colour to any tropical garden.

A mountain retreat

The rich red soil of the New South Wales village of Mount Wilson, a volcanic outcrop at one end of the Blue Mountains, supports some of Australia's best gardens. At this time of year, log fires are sending spires of smoke into the cool mountain air, as leaves of European trees turn red, orange and gold. Just wandering the lanes of this tiny mountain retreat, peering over established hedges to century-old exotic trees, is exciting. The gardens, often open to garden lovers, are both educational and inspirational.

Bebeah, a classic timber cottage with attic rooms and roofed with iron, was built in the 1880s for Edward Cox, a grazier from Rylstone, near Mudgee, and grandson of the pioneer William Cox. The house is now completely hidden from the road by 5 hectares of established gardens, beautifully restored by the designer Barry Byrne.

Vermilion-painted Chinese Chippendale gates beckon the visitor down the long sweeping drive, bordered on each side by immaculately clipped, small-leaved azaleas. Rare, deciduous trees that will soon be ablaze with colour, bend over the low and undulating hedge. An urn sits, completely at home, in a clipped green 'alcove' to the left of the drive; here, in winter, tall grasses add movement to the formal scene.

Guarding the house at the end of the drive is a massive copper beech; on the lawn to the other side of the house is a scarlet oak, its 30-metre spread supported by poles. From the front of the house, which is decorated in spring with the yellow banksian rose, you cross a wide lawn and pass the first dogwood to be planted in Australia, imported from America last century. A long iron arbor leads to plantings of more than 9000 azaleas, an extraordinary sight year-round, but particularly in early October when thousands more bluebells bloom.

Close to the house, the detail of the plantings, retained by exquisite dry stone walls, deserves very close inspection. Here, a delightful chapel has been restored and a parterre, planted with three different ivies, is exquisite. Past the house, a cherry walk leads on to the formal rose garden. A semi-circle of white and pink flowering *Camellia sasanqua* was planted three years ago, and is growing rapidly in the basalt soil and wonderful rainfall. Regular clipping has prevented the camellias from becoming 'leggy'.

Beyond is the lake with its vignettes of clever planting; there is *Cotoneaster horizontalis* clambering over local rock, along with punctuation points of *Agave americana* 'Mediopicta', and spires of cream and yellow *Kniphofia* against the backdrop of mountain trees.

Further on, a stone bridge leads to a Barry Byrne folly, a temple which, with plantings of hundreds of rhododendron, is part of a grand plan that is the work of an artist and art historian.

Guests can stay in an exquisitely restored cottage in this beautiful garden. Set in its own separate area, the cottage, with its stone floored conservatory, looks over the valley crowded with ancient tree ferns (*Cyathea australis*), a sign of an even older garden, created by nature.

'I've spent every day of the past eight years in this garden,' says Barry, who also advises that 'knowing when to stop with features' is all-important. 'Topiary is next,' he admits, somewhat irreverently. 'Whether or not it will be rabbits or chickens I'm not sure.'

Opposite: Woodland wonder at Bebeah.

Below: Bebeah, a classic timber cottage with attic rooms and an iron roof, was built in the 1880s.

Bottom left: Sunrise lights the garden.

How this garden works

* At Bebeah, hedges of clipped *Camellia sasanqua* form dense screens for creating structure, protection and privacy.

* 'Don't buy one or two of anything,' says Barry Byrne. 'Buy dozens. Even in a small garden you need to be greedy to achieve natural looking drifts.'

* Some of the rhododendron at Bebeah have been made into trees by underclipping and pruning out the lower branches to create a dramatic structure of twisted stems.

A romance in a garden

Graham and Lesley Cooke's garden is so successful that it might appear to the visitor, at first glance, maintenance free. A closer look reveals, however, that these are clever plantsmen and that this is a very disciplined garden. The success of the garden lies in both the selection of the plant material and the restraint with which the Cookes choose those plants. His motto, says Graham, is 'repetition and simplicity'.

Romantic Cottage Gardens is at Dromana, about an hour's drive from Melbourne. Ten hectares are taken up with landscape gardens, the nursery and the retail outlet.

'Structure is the most important element in the design of any garden,' says Graham. 'You have to create the structure first; once you get that right, then comes the plant combining.'

His garden is divided into several areas, with brick-edged paths defining the structure. The central walk is a perfect example of one of Graham's lessons in good design: the importance of mass planting. *Phlomis samia* flourishes, along with *Salvia* 'Indigo Spires' and, toward the front, *Nepeta* 'Walker's Blue'. Graham prefers this catmint, which he imported from the United Kingdom some five years ago, to 'Six Hills Giant' as it is more compact, and more floriferous. The blues here are offset with the feathery silver foliage of *Artemisia* 'Powis Castle'. The border is made up of multiples of just four plants. 'I know I have to choose,' says Graham. 'As much as I love plants I can't have everything.'

You turn down another path to a rich tapestry of blacks, deep greens, burgundies and purples; there is *Plectranthus oertendahlii* along with the tall-growing and trendy *Geranium maderense*. The dark-leaved *Helleborus foetidus* is offset by the exciting burgundy leaves of

'Elizabeth', a tall campanula with deep pink pendulant bells. 'A lot of campanulas are weak in the stem,' says Graham, 'but "Elizabeth" stands up, and she thrives in the sun, unlike most campanulas which are shy of flowering in the heat.'

The flexibility afforded by planting with perennials provides another lesson at Romantic Cottage Gardens. 'If you decide you want to change a perennial border, you can do it from one year to the next,' says Graham. 'You have to get it right the first time with shrubs.'

Opposite: Structure in the borders and mass plantings are essential in making this garden work.

Left: A canopy of the local *Eucalyptus viminalis* is created for a border of *Phlomis samia*, Salvia 'Indigo Spires' and *Nepeta* 'Walker's Blue'.

Below: *Heuchera* 'Black Pudding' to the front of the border, *Plectranthus oertendahlii* and *Helleborus foetidus* are all backed with the tall-growing *Geranium maderense*.

Heuchera 'Black Pudding', which forms a successful ground cover to the front of the border.

Graham loves the sedums, with their range of rusty colours so perfect for autumn. 'They are such robust plants, and they take no care. When we redesigned the garden, the sedums were taken out and left lying in a pile. They flowered their hearts out for two years without a care in the world. And they mass up so that you can divide them easily. *Sedum* "Autumn Joy" is a real comedian of a plant as it changes colour from this candy pink to a russet brown.'

New releases of imports are always adding excitement to the list at Romantic Cottage Gardens. This year there are four new sedums, including 'Purple Emperor', 'Sunset Cloud', and 'Green Expectation', bringing the number of good sedums on offer to twenty.

Lots of grasses, both tall and low growing, are used throughout the borders. The grasses, along with the sedums, add colour and rustle to the garden during winter; in cold climates, snow and frost provide an extra dimension by creating beautiful silhouettes. In the same group, the low growing carexes—'Bowles Golden', 'Frosted Curls' and 'Evergold'—are sensational on corners and at the front of the border.

Other new plants in the garden include *Campanula takesimana*

How this garden works

* While *Artemisia* 'Powis Castle' is a great silver-foliaged plant, it can go mad. Don't leave prunings around to provide mulch, for they grow so easily from cuttings, that you may find other treasures have been swamped! Cut back hard after frost, or replant each year.

* Sedums and grasses should be cut back when the new growth appears in spring.

* Grahame Cooke says that *Salvia* 'Indigo Spires' must be clipped when young, otherwise it will put up two or three long stems and not bush up.

Belmont

Gardeners are passionate people. Some would say obsessive. What could induce a sensible person—after a hard week of 'real' work—to spend weekends knee-deep in manure, with hands in compost, and to pour one's hard-earned, meagre wages into that never satisfied mistress, the garden?

You could suppose it's the thrill of creating something, the joy of seeing things grow, or the excitement of the turning seasons. At historic Belmont, in northern Tasmania, Carlton Cox says it is the sense that all is right with the world. 'I was raised in the garden, spent my childhood there, so it's a wonderful association for me. It's happy, tranquil. It's my retreat and thinking space.'

Eleven year old John Pascoe Fawkner arrived to settle ill-fated Port Phillip Bay in 1803, with his convict father, sister and mother, on board the H.M.S. *Calcutta*, which carried 308 convicts. With other convicts and free settlers, the family was soon moved to Van Diemen's Land.

Yet, by 1806, the Fawkners held a 50-acre land grant, soon to be extended with further grants to John. As a result of sharp practice, the eager John was incarcerated himself; he moved north to Launceston for a fresh start and married a former convict, Eliza Cobb, on 5 December, 1822. In 1823, Fawkner bought land that had been granted to a Simeon Smith the year before, and built the first section of Belmont, a cottage that still stands, attached to the main house.

Fawkner's many businesses and talents, all self-taught, included being a nurseryman. In 1828, he started the *Launceston Advertiser*, which he used to lampoon those who slighted him. After several attempts, Fawkner returned to Port Phillip Bay in 1835 to be part of the founding of Melbourne.

Belmont had been bought by Dr William Paton, for many years the president of the Horticultural Society, and a lecturer in horticulture. His tenure was seminal to the development of the property. The grand house that stands today was built by adding two wings to the original cottage. The mature exotic trees, the three massive English oaks in front of the house, the English ash, the deodars and the Scots pine date to at least this time.

After having several owners, the property was bought in 1942 by Reginald Cox, great grandson of the woolgrower and merchant James Cox, who built the great Georgian house, Clarendon, in 1838. James was the second son of William Cox, who built the first road over the Blue Mountains.

Descendants Robin Cox and her family have used photographic records from early this century for their work at Belmont. As no records exist to detail planting in the earliest garden, her son, Carlton, insists that their work is not of restoration. The garden would have been smaller than its present 2.5 hectares, and remnant fruit trees show that over

half was dedicated to providing food. In 1865 Belmont was advertised for rent in the *Launceston Examiner* and boasted 'extensive gardens including a quality orchard'.

'The house needed to sit in a more generous space—and because it has its own character, we wanted to have the ornamental garden away from the house. You need to go beyond to find the colour,' says Carlton.

'One of the key elements of the garden is the provision of several directions at every turn. We've tried to create a feeling of mystery. The visitor must choose,' he says.

Opposite: An entrance gate is dressed with roses.

Above: Historic Belmont at Longford.

Left: Interesting garden beds are now being created.

Garden ancestry

From a child I was always fond of a garden,' said Mrs Rolph Boldrewood in the preface to her book *The Flower Garden in Australia*, published in 1893, and the first Australian gardening book written by a woman. 'I have often changed residence, but always formed a garden, leaving it for others at our departure,' she wrote. 'To live without a garden would be for me an impossibility.'

Her direct descendant, garden designer Virginia Berger, also grew up surrounded by gardens; her mother has a much documented and photographed garden on Sydney's North Shore. When Virginia and her navy husband Paul bought their 1930s Canberra house 17 years ago, the garden was overgrown; privacy had been a major concern of the previous owners. Huge pine trees at the front of the property, which were out of proportion with the low house, were removed to allow in light and winter sun.

'I like to go into an old, overgrown, run-down garden and pull it to pieces,' says Virginia. 'You have to be ruthless. My mother says her garden is not a convalescent home. Anything that's not working goes. You can't achieve a good design if you retain something that's wrong. And you can always put things back.'

'You need to look at a garden you may have inherited to ascertain the main feature,' she says. In her small town garden, Virginia inherited a bold, sweeping wall; the strong line is accentuated today by an edge of closely clipped box. 'That wall has dictated the design of the entire garden,' she explains.

The back garden has been totally enclosed with plants. 'I believe that a successful garden is one that pleases, looking out from the house, no matter what the season. So form is all-important in this garden—far more so than plant material.'

Many of the plants in Virginia's garden are evergreen, and lend themselves to severe clipping, accentuating the strong design of the garden. Walls and fences have been clothed in clipped climbing fig or in *Camellia sasanqua*. Cotoneaster has been clipped into an arch, and clipped spheres and cones lend importance to the low box hedges which edge garden beds.

Toward the rear of the property is a secret garden, which you enter through a deep hedge of *Viburnum tinus*. Walls are covered with espaliered pears; a door covered with a mirror which reflects the other plant material in the garden gives an illusion of depth.

'Any glassmaker can make you a mirror, sealed for outdoors. Ask someone to hold it up to capture the best reflection. Once the mirror is in position, find a decorative iron gate to place over it.'

Another mirror is set into a tiny alcove by the front door. Reflecting the layers of green in the garden, it creates a sense of stepping through a much larger space.

Restraint is all important in the gardens Virginia designs. 'It's a mistake to try to have too many things in a garden. A friend calls them "pizza gardens"—with a bit of everything.'

'Gardening is interior decorating for the outside,' she says. 'People go to great lengths to decorate a house, to have colours that go together—but this is just as important in the garden.'

Opposite: A bold line forms the backbone of the Berger garden.

Below: Clipped spheres emphasise the strong lines in the garden.

Left: The colours of the *Liquidamber styraciflua* are found in the garden during autumn.

Invergowrie

During autumn the Northern Tablelands of New South Wales are awash with colour, which continues until the end of April and often into May. The area is also steeped in history—the history of land settlement in New South Wales, of pastoral and of garden history.

In the 1840s a group of men moved north from Sydney and took up several runs, each of tens of thousands of acres. Governor Gipps became concerned with the power of these squatters and introduced bills to curb their wealth. One of those runs was Saumarez, and it was on part of this run that James Mitchell settled in the 1860s, building Invergowrie, and surrounding it with a detailed homestead garden. His great grandson, Doug Moffatt, is restoring this important garden with the assistance of botanist Ian Telford.

The garden today is seen against the backdrop of mature, original radiata pines which were planted as an entrance avenue and as windbreaks. The original entrance to the house, and the fences which defined the garden from the surrounding grazing property, are being restored. 'You come outside the fence and look into the garden proper, to contemplate the garden from a different aspect; then walk on, and back into the garden,' says Telford.

In front of the ochre-painted weatherboard house an original box hedge protects a garden designed around a diamond pattern, and edged with original terracotta tiles. The arrangement of this garden of heritage roses, herbs and other perennials sympathetic to the time, is geometric, following the advice of J. C. Loudon, the most influential writer of the early nineteenth century who was recommending a geometric style for 'gardens in the wild'.

Opposite left: Pergolas and walkways divide the garden.

Opposite right: Perennial borders along the side of the house.

Left: A shaded walk.

Below: One of the outbuildings at Invergowrie.

Ian Telford has designed the garden to display a range of colours at any one time. At the eastern end of the front garden the purple and bronze colours of the berberis and smoke bush tone with the burnt-orange of tiger lilies. Above is a golden ash, annually gearing up for its autumn show. The yellows and purples graduate to the reds and pinks of the roses, which are underplanted with blues and silver-leaved plants.

The iris, which flower first in spring, team with the lilacs in October, and the groundcovers of forget-me-nots, thymes, campanulas and pulmonarias. The replantings of old roses, including 'Mme Lombard', 'La France', 'Lady Hillingdon' and 'Mme Louis Leveque', are based on a 1919 planting list of the owner's grandfather.

At the western end of the front garden the colours move into white, represented by *Viburnum plicatum* 'Mariesii', with its spreading, horizontal arms. You leave the white garden by an arch of two white wisteria.

The owners believe that a good garden is one that looks a bit too much to handle. 'And with too much money you go too fast; it's better to spend time thinking about the best way to do things,' says Doug Moffatt.

On the northern side of the house are two funeral cypress (*Chamaecyparis funebris*) and two old, large photinia, planted in classic Victorian fashion, as two pairs. Along the verandah here is a shaded border of the covetted giant lily (*Cardiocrinum giganteum*), the large-leaved *Gunnera manicata* and hellebores, partly edged with tiles thought to have been made on site.

On the eastern side of the house is a large and important vegetable garden, designed classically, in straight lines, east–west, and housing a replanting of original 'Isabella' grapes.

How this garden works

* Protect early plantings from damaging winds with shadecloth barriers which can be removed later.

* Ian Telford's advice, when restoring an old garden, is: 'Don't stick rigidly to one point in time; choose the best of each generation'.

* Doug Moffatt always advises, 'go slowly. Don't try to do too much too quickly'.

Southern light

The works of Sir Hans Heysen and of his daughter, Nora, are given perspective by a visit to his house and garden. The garden, which is bursting with old roses and perennials, sits within a quintessentially Australian landscape of river red gums (*Eucalyptus camaldulensis*) and white gums (*E. rubida*), which Hans Heysen loved to paint. Both he and Nora drew heavily on the garden for their work: he is quoted in *The Home* magazine of December 1921 as saying, 'I don't want to paint human beings: they do not appeal to me in the way animals and Nature do'.

The Cedars, built in 1878, was bought by the Heysen family in 1912. Sir Hans Heysen painted here until he died in 1968, and the property is now owned by his grandchildren.

The garden, full of charm and spirit throughout the year, is perhaps at its best in autumn when the delicate colours of the apple blossom japonica (*Chaenomeles japonica*) are offset by the vibrant autumn foliage.

The large collection of roses throughout the garden includes a Heysen favourite, 'Marjorie Palmer', a rose bred in 1936 by Alister Clark, and is planted amongst delphiniums, penstemons, species gladioli and his beloved dahlias. Other favourite roses were 'Frau Karl Druschki', 'Snow Queen', bred in 1901 (also known as the 'Scentless Beauty'), the generous 'Duchesse de Brabant', 'Mme Ernst Calvat', a sport of the deep pink, very scented, Bourbon 'Mme Isaac Pereire' and 'Souvenir de la Malmaison' which loves the hot and dry climate of South Australia.

Nora Heysen also drew heavily on the garden for her flower paintings in oil, and was particularly fond of 'Mme Isaac Pereire' and her father's favourite rose, 'Malmaison', which does so well in the hot and dry climate of South Australia.

Hans Heysen's studio was built away from the house and faces south so that he could capture the southern—not direct—light for his painting. It was built at vast expense (£400 in 1912) was designed by an architect and took local builders six months to construct. Hans Heysen painted in the studio for 55 years.

Nora's studio, where she painted in the 1930s and 1940s, was created from the charming stone stables, close to the house. A skylight, which was added for the superb southern light, and its jarrah flooring have now been restored.

The Cedars is cared for by custodian Allan Campbell, a horticulturalist who has also completed a two-year Master's thesis on the artist, and who conducts tours of the house and the artist's studio. Allan agrees that his favourite time in the garden is in late April and early May. 'Then, the autumn colours make a wonderful contrast with the surrounding gums,' he says.

Top left: Nora Heysen's studio at The Cedars.

Top right Strong stonework is softened with plantings of erigeron.

Water-wise gardening

The year 1998 brought the worst drought in some 20 years; it was becoming clear, even to those of us who hankered after the soft and pretty colours of the English gardens, that water-wise plants are unavoidable in this country.

Even the so-called 'hill station' gardens in the highlands and mountain areas around Australia were losing established trees if owners turned their backs for an instant. In the country, dams were almost empty and the lucky souls who had springs and bores were finding that watertables had risen dramatically and the quality of the water had dropped.

At Barrabool Hills Maze and Gardens at Ceres, near Geelong in Victoria, owners Jenny Smith and her son, Richard Seccull, realised some years ago that endless watering was not going to be possible forever.

Jenny visited the gardens of the south of France and of Italy in 1989, and loved the clever planting combinations used at gardens such as La Mortola, an Italian garden of some 45 hectares almost on the border between France and Italy. 'The gardens of the Mediterranean and the Riviera understand the use of gravel, running water and succulents,' she says. 'You can plant echiveras, aloes, agaves and coltylens cleverly. In front of, say, purple flax, for contrast, these plants look great.' The variegated cordylines, *Cordyline fruticosa* 'Tricolor', with its pink and cream colourings and *Cordyline fruticosa* 'Imperialis', its dark green leaves streaked pink and crimson, also look effective.

When they created their 5-hectare, terraced garden, Jenny and Richard concentrated on scree, or gravel gardens using shallow-rooted plants that are not thirsty. There are echiveras, which look marvellous as they cover the ground with their grey rosettes and require virtually no water. The aloes provide stunning punctuation points and the drought-tolerant red hot pokers (*Kniphofia* spp.) provide drama and colour. There is the apricot-coloured *K.* 'Princess Beatrix', *K.* 'Percy's Pride', with its green flowers and the bright orange *K.* 'Winter Cheer'. Also stunning is *K. ensifolia*, which sports huge yellow flower heads in winter. According to Jenny, the kniphofias are easy to look after. 'Just cut the stems back after flowering and lift and divide every four years,' she says.

The echiums are also great value, requiring little water or maintenance, but providing months of drama and colour in winter. (They are cut back each year after flowering; take care not to cut into hard wood.)

The garden houses two fascinating mazes, sited on each side of the terraces. The first is created of the traditional cypress, *Cupressus macrocarpa*, and is five years old. There is also a marvellous circular maze created from one of Edna Walling's favourite plants *Teucrium fruticans*. The grey-leaved plants are the least thirsty and the grey of the *Teucrium* looks most effective here, bordered with a long pergola covered in roses, including the dark red 'Black Boy', bred by Victorian rose grower Alister Clark.

The *rugosa* species of roses is also water-wise and a long hedge of *Rosa rugosa* 'Rosarie de l'Hay', bordering the pergola, leads down to a lake which provides the backdrop to the entire, terraced garden. Around the house the clear-red single flowers of the climbing rose 'Altissimo' provide a perfect counterpoint for the greys throughout the garden.

Below: A scarcity of water should be no hindrance to growing a garden of complex beauty, as is evident at Barabool Hills Maze and Gardens at Ceres, near Geelong.

Cool climate treasures

The rolling hills behind Adelaide, like so many of the mountain areas that back the seaboard capitals, support 'hill station' gardens that bring to mind a colonial era of misty English light, intense greens and golden afternoons. These ambitious gardens that were created by the city merchants some 100 years ago, and that suitably displayed their wealth and standing, are now reaching maturity, and remain for modern garden lovers to enjoy.

It is difficult to dismiss our earliest pioneers' love of grand gardens with spreading English trees as simply being early pretentions to the symbols of a class to which they could only aspire at home in England. As late as 1869, artists such as Louis Buvelot were painting eucalypts with the form of English oaks. Those shapes and colours still inspire us today to lust after the 'exotics' and struggle with plants we shouldn't even think about growing.

Gardens are emblematic of taste and culture in any society and a growing or changing garden style also indicates changes in social and economic times. While we might sympathise with our first settlers who created Arcadian visions, a garden style that is unique to this varied landscape is developing in the late twentieth century.

Garden historian and author Trevor Nottle, who gardens at Stirling in the Adelaide Hills, is adamant that we can't continue to pine for the saturated greens of England. 'The place we have chosen to live can only be the place it is,' he says. 'As gardeners we must try to make it as beautiful as possible within sensible environmental limits that take full account of the patterns of landscape, the rhythm of the seasons, the flow of local weather patterns and the tempo and cycle of growth. This means accepting the rough brown land, the summer drought, the torrential downpours, the beauty of winter and the flat yellowness of grasses aestivating through summer.'

'There is no requirement to deny our past,' continues Nottle, 'but it's stifling to make continual backward-looking references to it, as in most current garden design. To know where we are now, to explore all the possibilities, of both exotic and native plants, and to move on—that surely is the way forward.'

Each autumn, however, one can't help being extremely glad that our early gardeners planted beautiful cold climate trees that are now swaggering with autumn colour. Mount Lofty Botanic Garden, at Piccadilly in the Adelaide Hills, is one garden devoted to the cultivation of the world's cool temperate plants; it was displaying particularly glorious autumn colour. The reds of the pin oaks (*Quercus palustris*), the yellows of the ashes, the gingkos and the tulip trees (*Liriodendron tulipifera*) lit the hillsides.

Opened in 1977, Mount Lofty is made up of seven intersecting gullies; each has a specific planting theme.

Rhododendron Valley, which culminates in the Duck Pond, becomes a mass of colour in spring. The pond is surrounded with impressive plantings of brilliantly-coloured mollis azaleas, and of *Gunnera manicata*, the giant ornamental rhubarb, which thrives in the moist conditions. (*Gunnera* benefits from a protective mulch when dormant in winter.)

To walk through Fern Gully, which houses over 500 fern species, both native and exotic, that are established under a canopy of the native messmate (*Eucalyptus obliqua*) is like entering another world and is fascinating at any time of the year.

The Rock Garden overlooks a small lake with iris planted on its banks and merges into the much-loved Woodland Garden. From here two streams lead to several waterfalls and to a bog garden.

Magnolia Gully is a breathtaking sight in early spring. 'We have over 40 different species of magnolia, including *Magnolia campbellii*, with its luscious pink blooms,' says Mount Lofty's Chris Steele-Scott. 'When in full bloom in August, Magnolia Gully looks as though a flock of white doves has descended.'

Opposite: *Gunnera manicata* thrives on the edges of the Duck Pond in Mount Lofty Botanic Garden, at Piccadilly in the Adelaide Hills.

Bottom left: *Rhododendron* 'Loderi Venus'.

Bottom right: The soft colours of *R.* 'Helene Schiffner'.

The good oil

About an hour from Perth is New Norcia, Australia's only monastic town and a place of great calm and serenity. New Norcia was founded in 1846 by a small group of Benedictine monks headed by Dom Rosendo Salvado, to whom the government lent 180 000 hectares of land to pioneer a new style of mission.

A visit to New Norcia is not just a visit to a set of unusual buildings in a wonderful landscape; it is also an experience of the hospitality of the Benedictine community. 'A visit to the town is a visit to us,' says Dom Christopher Power who, as Prior and procurator, looks after the day to day running of the community.

Around the town is the community's farm, 8500 hectares that support wheat and sheep. There is also the now-famous bread, there are fruit and vegetables, and the community runs the New Norcia hotel.

All the buildings were designed and built by the monks. The earliest part of the Abbey Church is a simple Georgian looking structure, built in 1847. Spanish style additions were made at the turn of the century,

under the direction of Abbot Torres who, as well as being the second Abbot, was an architect. The avenue in front of the monastery is lined with white cedar (*Melia azedarach*), a popular shade tree for dry climates. The scented lilac flowers are followed by berries, greatly loved by the birds but poisonous to humans.

New Norcia is the setting for all manner of conferences, workshops, music festivals, and camps. 'We have 40 school visits a year and over half of them are music camps. We've had the girls playing the bagpipes up and down the road,' says Dom Chris.

In 1866 an olive grove was planted with 400 cuttings; 250 still survive using only traditional Mediterranean methods of production. 'In 1997, the Community joined forces with the University of Western Australia to rejuvenate the New Norcia olive trees and develop a quality protocol for New Norcia Olive Oil,' says Dom Chris.

Around New Norcia is the largest area of remnant vegetation in Western Australia. 'The early monks cleared very intelligently so that 4000 hectares of bushland is largely untouched. Some of the areas are being revegetated and corridors formed to make the natural heritage more available to visitors,' says Dom Chris. 'Walk trails will go past various parts of the farm and points of historic interest. But we have to balance that with being farmers too; the farm is our main asset. We must be earners of income.

'In the old days the community was large and almost exclusively Spanish. The monks came to Australia having received a very broad education in Spain. One, Father William Gimenez, had studied botany at Monserrat monastery and started the New Norcia herbarium when he arrived in 1908. Every Wednesday he would go into the bush, pick the wildflowers and write them up. That is how we know what was there.'

Most visitors are well able to understand the uniqueness of the place. While other monastic settlements have merged with the local town, because New Norcia is a certain distance from Perth and because the Benedictine community owns everything around the town, it has been able to preserve the place as the expression of one community's history over 152 years.

Left: St Gertrude's, a former convent in New Norcia, holds workshops and conferences.

Treasure hunting

Tasmania occupies a crucial place in our pastoral, architectural, literary and gardening heritage. The state boasts some of Australia's earliest buildings, many of them exceptionally beautiful, convict-built private houses; it is also the site of the most extraordinary scenery. Some of our best nurseries are in Tasmania; one of them is Elizabeth Town Nursery. Many an Australian garden is stocked with plants from this nursery, and has been created with advice given by the nursery's owners, John and Corrie Dudley.

The 0.5 hectare nursery and display garden is arranged in order of its collections of cool-climate plants, and only the most strong-willed traveller could resist the rare finds. If you're taking your car on the ferry from Melbourne—an adventure in itself—there is no need to resist, and the nursery is en route from the Devonport depot to Launceston.

The nursery is well-known for its alpine treasures. Corrie's advice for growing these somewhat tricky plants is 'give them natural conditions as much as possible. Alpines like shallow soil, perfect drainage and full sun'.

Elizabeth Town Nursery also offers collections of primula, iris, paeonia, hosta and clematis. The nursery is perhaps most famous for its collection of *Helleborus*, including *H. orientalis* 'Mrs Betty Ranicar', a rare double white, discovered by the Dudleys and named for a noted and much-loved local gardener. 'Betty Ranicar' will flower all summer, and even does well in Sydney gardens, in filtered sunlight.

Among the collections of iris, is the beautiful Japanese iris (*I. ensata*) with their delicate stripes of blues and pinks. There is also the tiny *Iris cristata* which forms dense clumps. 'It's very easy as long as it has full sun and perfect drainage,' says Corrie. 'It does well in northern gardens as it likes a warmer climate than that of Tasmania.'

There are covetous displays of *Primula* x *pubescens*, commonly called auriculas; the flowers of intense colours appear to be edged with chalk. They thrive in the perfect drainage provided by Corrie's home-made stone-look troughs.

Above: *Primula* at Elizabeth Town Nursery.

Feng shui

We probably all agree that gardens should promote a sense of peace and serenity. There are more than a handful of us, however, who look at our gardens only with a rising sense of panic at the work still to be done, and muse on why the weeds grow better than anything else.

On the far north coast of New South Wales is a garden of balance and harmony, where Eastern spirituality and the principles of good garden design and 'garden keeping' combine to create a haven of ordered tranquility.

Elizabeth Crawford is a *feng shui* consultant who moved north from Sydney, taking with her a need for peace, a love of Eastern gardens, and some precious pieces of granite sculpture. 'I had been in China visiting some of the very old gardens, and wanted to create the same sense of peace,' she says.

Faced with a space that was a 'typical suburban backyard' she asked garden designer Tim Hays, also an import from Sydney, for help.

Tim has created walkways and vistas to best site the granite pieces. 'Elizabeth had quite strong ideas on where her sculpture should go,' says Tim. 'Once we had our focal points in place, according to *feng shui* principles, we made the garden work around those key points.'

For Elizabeth, the Chinese goddess Quan Yin is the centre of the garden. 'We placed her first; then the whole energy of the garden shifted around. Everything is placed in relationship to her. The garden is

supporting the *feng shui*, the energy, of the house,' she explains. 'In other words, what I've done in the garden supports the energy inside the house. The energy pattern in a house is determined by the year it is built, by its position, how it sits on the land, among other things.'

Paths meander throughout to create the illusion of a much larger garden. 'Also, in *feng shui*, straight paths are pathways for the negative energy, *shaqi*, as the energy travels too quickly. *Sheng qi* is positive energy. When you curve a pathway to slow the movement you get the beneficial energy from it. That's why it always feels better to wander.'

At the apex of each path is an important tree. Existing rainforest trees, such as the kurrajong (*Brachychiton acerifolius*) were left, and the overall scheme developed around them. There is also the beautiful euodia, a local rainforest tree of the coast and the mountains that bears showy pink flowers throughout summer.

Soil preparation was crucial. The existing soil was either removed completely and replaced, or aerated with a mini-excavator, and the local red, volcanic soil was further enriched with chicken manure. 'The whole thing ends up soft and friable and the plants grow very quickly,' says Tim.

'I always emphasise groundcovers because here in the sub-tropics the weeding is a nightmare.' Beds which divide the winding paths are packed with plant material. *Ctenanthe oppenheimiana*, with its fascinating leaves with purple undersides, masses out quickly to become an effective groundcover. False heather (*Cuphea hyssopifolia*) is a tough groundcover that is covered in cream flowers from spring to winter. The leopard lily (*Belamcanda chinensis*) grows close to the ground; once a year, in summer, it sends up spires of spotted flowers. Tim also likes to use the scented spider lily (*Hymenocallis* x *festalis*) from South America.

Just outside the back door of the house is a Japanese water bowl, in a setting of bamboo and local palms. According to Elizabeth, 'Water represents wealth and prosperity, so you want to place water in an area that is going to activate the prosperity stars that are in the house.'

Opposite: The studio is placed according to the principles of feng shui.

Above: A sense of calm is enhanced by the gentle sound of water.

Left: An outdoor shower surrounded by nature.

How this garden works

* In Tim Hays' gardens, tea-tree mulch is used as 'it's a local product, looks good, and is quite cheap'.

* The spider lily quickly multiplies, the congestion hampering flowering. It is easily divided, after flowering, by lifting with a garden fork, and breaking the bulbs apart or by slicing into the clump with a medium-sized kitchen knife.

* In Chinese gardens four components—water, rocks, buildings and plants—combine to create peace and harmony.

Cooinda

Di Maune's garden, Cooinda, looks much older than its eight years. Set in 9 hectares near the northern New South Wales town of Moree, the garden owes its established look to a protective backdrop of inherited, massive, river red gums (*Eucalyptus camaldulensis*) which tower over it and hug the bank of the Mehi River, which runs through the magnificent property.

The canopy of the eucalypts provides the flower borders with protection from frosts which drop to −4°C, and from heat which reaches over 40°C. 'Bougainvillea is used a lot in this climate,' says Di. 'It's spectacular, and flowers best when it's doing it tough.'

The steep bank to the river is terraced, to make it workable, and covered with ivy-leaved geranium. A very pale pink valerian (*Centranthus ruber*) also grows here in wide swathes.

Di Maune's background as a florist is evident in the arrangement of plant material in the main border. *Tecoma capensis*, with its yellow flowers in autumn, tones with, and is sheltered by, a golden elm. In the background is *Euphorbia rigida*, with its lime-green leaves and yellow flower heads. The use of various greys throughout softens the garden.

The garden has expanded as Di found more plants she couldn't live without. 'The garden is a lot larger than my husband intended,' admits Di. 'One evening, I got a man to take a fence out. When I got up the next morning, the fence was back.'

'I like the garden to be flowing and natural, except near the house where beds are planted out in pinks and white, with a touch of blue,' she says. 'The mass plantings of pale pink ranunculus can be frustrating—suddenly a red and an orange one will come through and you

daisies and petunias decorating the courtyard; the pots must be protected by bark, when the garden is not open for visitors.

Opposite: The magnificent garden at Cooinda.

Left: The rose 'Chicago Peace'.

Below: The rose 'Queen Elizabeth'.

have to quickly whip it out. *Alstroemeria* are wonderful in a hot climate, and are very easy to grow,' she adds. She plants a pale pink form with a very double, pale pink *Pelargonium* called 'Always'. Another favourite is *Ballota pseudodictamnus*, with its apple-green foliage, which Di uses in cut flower arrangements as it 'looks very natural and lasts forever'.

A walkway lined with poles of wisteria and roses leads under an arch of the rose 'Wedding Day' and through a pergola of the rose 'Albertine', a mass of pink in late October, planted with the recurrent apricot-coloured rose 'Meg' to extend the flowering season. The rose garden is divided into beds, according to colour. In the pale pink bed is 'Bridal Pink', 'Flamingo' and 'Peach Blossom'; the deeper pink bed houses 'Queen Elizabeth', 'Chicago Peace' and 'Tiffany'. There are beds of reds, of apricots and of yellows, while beds of the white roses 'Pristine', 'Pascali' and 'Iceberg' encircle the rose garden. In its centre is a circular bed of standard weeping *Rosa* 'New Dawn'.

The property grows the Chinese Empress tree (*Paulownia tomentosa*) for its beautiful wood which is used for cabinet making. The tree can be milled for softwood after five years or as hardwood after seven.

The peacocks which strut the garden, preening themselves in the glass picture windows of the house, can play havoc with the pots of

How this garden works

* Di Maune designs her garden beds by laying out hoses, and moving them around until the shape is just right.

* Covering the ground with plant material is essential for weed suppression. At Cooinda, dense groundcovers are provided by a pink-flowered ivy-leaved geranium and the aluminium plant (*Lamium maculatum* 'Roseum').

Mistydowns

While many of us are fighting off the first bout of flu of the cooler weather, and avoiding cutting back summer borders 'till next week', Mistydowns in Victoria's Western District is dressing up for a marvellous display of autumn roses.

The Western District, the site of some of Australia's best grazing and agricultural land, is also home to some of our greatest gardens. Cattle graze quietly in green paddocks under those most Australian of trees, the river red gums, (*Eucalyptus camaldulensis*), much-loved by the painters of the so-called Heidelberg School. The Grampians, razor-sharp, rugged and an intense blue, provide an extraordinary backdrop to many of the gardens in the area.

Mistydowns is a one-hectare terraced garden based around roses and perennials as well as rare bulbs. Tea roses—the first to bloom and the last to finish—are now in full flower; they are not pruned until late each year, when the danger of damaging late frosts are finished. The extensive collection of teas include the beautiful 'Baronne Henriette de Snoy' with its wonderful red stems and its relaxed, very double flowers, the colours of aged silk. There is also 'Catherine Mermet', 'Monsieur Tillier' and the luscious, white, 'Mrs Herbert Stevens'.

Owner, Judy Morrison, has to be careful with water as rainfall is just 450 millimetres per year, and is unreliable. Ornamental ponds are used for irrigation and as a recycling system; all nursery water is collected in underground drains, before being filtered through two ponds into a holding dam for re-use on the garden. The garden is not watered for much of the year, however; only the tough survive. The entire garden is clay, and loads of topsoil have been brought in to the garden, with the result that digging has not been necessary. 'The roses love to get their feet down into the clay providing you give them mulch,' says Judy.

As well as a comprehensive collection of the roses of English grower, David Austin, Mistydowns houses a complete collection of the roses of Victorian rose breeder, Alister Clark. 'Being a man, he lent toward strong colour. So we have graded the roses from his soft tones to his bright reds,' says Judy, recounting how roses at Mistydowns are arranged for colour, rather than by type, thus creating a harmonious design rather than a museum of roses. Judy also has the full collection of the rugosa stock available in Australia.

The soft pink rose 'Stanwell Perpetual' is planted along the property's boundary fence, the pale green leaves toning with the glaucous leaves of the eucalypts in the fields in the distance. Sheep prune one side and the owners prune the other!

Beyond the fences, in a dry paddock, 45 'Leverkusen', the scented, yellow rose bred in 1954 by the German grower Kordes, flowers all summer on the dam bank, teaming with the dry landscape.

Opposite: Thick layers of mulch preserve moisture and add structure to the clay in the garden.

Above: Walkways of roses and perennials.

Left: Simple poles support the roses, including 'Scorcher' a clear-red hybrid tea.

How this garden works

* Always disinfect secateurs between rosebushes, whether pruning, 'dead-heading' or picking flowers for a vase. At Mistydowns, Judy Morrison uses two pairs of secateurs, so that one pair can rest in the disinfectant (she uses methylated spirits) for 10 minutes before re-use.

* The tea roses are pruned later, after the danger of frost is over.

Harmonious sculpture

An extended stay in Italy in the 1970s was a major influence on the work of sculptor Jan King. There she visited some of the great Italian gardens, developing her understanding of how sculpture can be used in the garden. Her words today are in harmony with those of designer Edna Walling, who believed that 'nature is the best teacher of all,' and of her disciple, Kath Carr, who admonished 'don't gild the lily'.

Jan King believes that placement is all-important. 'Sculpture can link the house and the landscape,' she says. 'Relate the scale of the work to the height and scale of the house.' She advises that the sculpture should also relate to a specific part of the house—a piece on a verandah, for instance, is the link between house and garden.

'The work will also relate to the lines of the house, or to the plantings in the garden. The horizontal line of lawn and terrace could be echoed in the choice of sculpture. A vertical piece looks wonderful in the midst of a stand of upright eucalypts or pencil pines.'

The work of Jan King and Paul Hopmeier graces some of Australia's best gardens—both large and small. In one large country garden, designed in the 1940s by Edna Walling, the curving lines of the large lake and the surrounding crabapples are reflected in the circles and curves of the sculpture Jan created.

When asked if people are frightened by sculpture, Jan says, 'They should talk to the artist who will have some thought about siting—he probably imagined the piece in a certain situation'. Jan loves to visit a client's garden to discuss where a piece may go. 'The placement becomes such a joy and the sculpture, in its site, starts to live,' she says. 'A lot of work is quiet—it doesn't have to be vast and intimidating,' she

shale. When they bought the property, on Sydney's lower North Shore, it was a mass of weeds. Weeks of hoeing were followed by covering the area in underfelt. Next, 15 centimetres of aged woodchip was laid, before tube-stock of the Australian cedar and Sydney blue gum was planted.

That Jan and Paul are influenced by nature is clearly evident in their work. 'I try to represent the stillness of nature,' says Jan. 'A small, salt-water rock pool is extraordinary—created as it was out of the force of the waves. Then comes such stillness.'

Opposite: *Melia* in slate and steel, by Jan King.

Left: *January* in steel, by Paul Hopmeier.

Below: *Leaping Sculpture* in steel, by Paul Hopmeier.

adds. 'Small sculpture is appropriate in a small area. It may be tucked into a corner, or it may be placed on a piece of stone in a courtyard garden, perhaps with a chair nearby for contemplation.'

Rather than have many pieces of inferior quality, 'it is better to have one good piece,' says Jan. 'You can tell if it's good—if it has a sense of form, a presence, if it's not cluttered.'

The garden around Jan and Paul's 1920s house is created in several different areas, each with a different feel. The front verandah is host to a small sculpture by Paul. In the back garden, a large jacaranda spreads over a larger piece of his work—the lines of the sculpture echo the branches of the tree.

The 15-metre square rainforest area of the garden has been re-created in an area that was the source of timber for colonial Sydney and on deep

How this garden works

* In a garden, a sculpture could be placed where a wall finishes— or against a blank wall. 'Give the work its own importance,' say Jan King.

* An element of surprise is important. Jan and Paul's rainforest garden is created with several secret places, connected by a winding path, and each home to a small work of art. You come around a corner to find a small sculpture.

Camellia paradise

The best advice a gardener will ever be given is that of Bob Cherry, collector of the genus *Camellia*, and breeder of many varieties of the *sasanqua* species of this beautiful flower. When asked the best conditions in which to grow camellias, he says, 'Look at the natural environment of any plant you are growing. Ask yourself how it grows in the wild'.

Over the past 25 years, Bob Cherry has created an inspirational 12-hectare garden, Paradise Plants, 300 metres above sea level at Kulnura on the Central Coast of New South Wales. As well as giving the gardening community many new camellias, Bob has introduced many glorious plants such as *Osmanthus* 'Pearly Gates' and *Gordonia* 'Harvest Moon', with its enormous pure white flowers.

'I always wanted to be a nurseryman,' he says when asked to define the appeal of gardening for him. 'Growing plants is all I ever wanted to do.' Bob takes regular plant-hunting trips to China and the warmer Vietnam, where he collects in the wild, with local government permission and supervision, choosing for form, flower and suitability for Australian conditions, providing new treasures for the avaricious collector market.

'The South Coast to mid North Coast of New South Wales would be the best climate in the world for growing the widest variety of species and forms of *Camellia*,' says Bob. 'The natural homeland for *Camellia sasanqua* is Southern Japan, which is on the same latitude as Sydney.'

Camellia japonica is also native to Japan, while most other camellia species are native to southern China, where the climate is similar to the south-east of Australia. The rare yellow camellia, *C. nitidissima*, (syn. *C. chrysantha*), is from south-eastern China and North Vietnam; it does well in Sydney and can be expected to thrive as far north as Cairns.

The ideal soil for growing camellias is acid, although many grow naturally on limestone. At Paradise Plants, the soil is, by Bob Cherry's admission, 'terrible, with everything from pure sandstone, to sand over rock to sandy loam to clay'.

The most important factor is the drainage of the soil; here, the beds are built up to ensure good drainage. The roots of the plants should be constantly cool and moist, and liberal use of mulch and organic matter is important. 'Remember that camellias in their natural state are forest plants and enjoy layers of leaf litter,' says Bob. He advises that the genus will grow equally well in sun or shade, provided the root area of the plant is kept cool and moist.

Bob fertilises his plants with a complete fertiliser once a year—'a handful per square metre of surface area for mature plants'.

Camellias are extremely generous, flowering from February to September. It would be reasonable to say, also, that there is a camellia for every occasion. They make marvellous low hedges, an interesting alternative to box. The Paradise varieties *Camellia sasanqua* 'Paradise Petite', 'Paradise Little Liane' and 'Paradise Baby Jane' are particularly suitable for clipping and will also grow happily in pots.

The small flowered hybrids such as 'Blondi' and 'Bogong Snow', which are white, and the white, flushed with pink 'Wirlinga Princess' have the form of small blossom trees, and bloom in winter and spring.

In a small garden or courtyard, where each plant chosen has to earn its keep, the currency of fragrance increases. Several of the species of camellia are scented, including *C. yuhsienensis*, *C. forrestii* and *C. lutchuensis*. There are also scented *Camellia japonica* varieties, such as 'Acksent', 'Scented Sun' and 'Super Scent' and 'Scentsation'. Some camellia species, including *C. crapnelliana* have the bonus of interesting bark.

Paradise Plants holds two open weekends each year and the Camellia Society is on hand to identify flowers. The society also stages a display of the most beautiful blooms imaginable. You can buy plants, and it's impossible to discipline yourself to choose between 'Mrs D. W. Davis', a pale, pale pink, the more flamboyant and ruffled 'Elegans Splendor' and 'Fimbriata', which is white with ruffled edges. There is also the peony-formed 'C. M. Wilson', the elegant 'Shiro Chan', the impossibly pretty 'Wilhemina Soper' and 'Chinese Lantin', restrained and beautiful.

Opposite: Paradise Plants offers perfect conditions for camellias.

Top left: *Camellia japonica* 'Martha Tuck'.

Below: *Gordonia* 'Harvest Moon'.

Claire Welsh's garden

Claire Welsh has loved the wildflowers of Western Australia since she was a child. Ten years ago she moved to Perth, where the garden had been established by pioneers in wildflower growing. She also inherited the extended garden of the Hollywood Reserve, just across the road.

Claire believes that when designing with native plants one needs to experiment. 'Mainly, you need to observe nature,' she says. Although she planned her garden, she maintains it is a bit eclectic, a bit random, a bit like nature. 'It's hard to define. Nature does not coordinate colours so the colours here are mixed. You need to keep in mind the ecological factors of the regions in which the plants appear naturally. You must think about soil types, climate. Do the plants need summer water? The thing is to plant species with similar needs together.' And the result is a great success. 'Even though one may be seduced and enchanted with the more delicate things, it's the toughies you'll have, in the end,' she adds.

'In my ignorance in my first hot summer here, I thought I could create a miniature sand plain-cum-coastal heathland in this garden. Apart from height and visibility problems, as it extended onto the verge, it didn't cope with the first winter when, for four months, it was in the shade cast by mature stone pines.'

The front garden has to be kept low, with sight lines for traffic and pedestrians in mind. Plants are kept to half a metre in height, which means they have to be replaced more often.

Some of the successful smaller plants are the cotton tops, *Conostylis aculeata*, the orange flame pea, *Chorizema cordatum*, and the prostrate dryandra, *Dryandra nivea*. There is also *Boronia crenulata* with its pink flowers, and the purple iris, *Pattersonia occidentalis*. Spring colour is

'There has inevitably been much trial and error,' she admits. 'There have been removals and replanting as my knowledge and understanding of the individual requirements in growing many Australian plants has developed. To know the plants well enough to be able to design with them intelligently is also a challenge and a skill acquired by observation, experience and a good dose of luck.'

Opposite: Glorious wildflowers abound in Claire Welsh's garden.

Left: *Chamelaucium ciliatum* 'Purple Pride'.

Below: The smoke bush *Conospermum eatoniae*.

added with the everlasting daisies in pink, white and yellow. 'They are easy to grow,' says Claire, 'provided you take precautions against snails and plant them in full sun.'

The new developments in plant selection have made previously difficult plants accessible, says Claire. 'There are innumerable new hybrid kangaroo paws in various sizes and colours, many of which flower almost continuously. And the spectacular blue *Dampiera eriocephala*, from the Stirling Ranges, has been tissue cultured and flowers on my verge for months.'

As gardening is about controlling nature, Claire Welsh admits that she compromises in the garden. 'If you were going totally natural, you wouldn't take out anything that dies. You'd leave it for the birds and insects, lizards and fungi, just as in nature.

'In old gardens there is an accumulation of pathogens and fungi that are not compatible with the roots of the more "fussy" plants growing naturally in the harshest of conditions, with no rainfall for at least six months of the year and usually in symbiosis with a particular fungus which helps to feed and keep them healthy. Those people who start out with a bush block of virgin land are indeed fortunate if they wish to have a native garden.

How this garden works

* Claire Welsh advises planting natives in new soil, where possible. Soil that is polluted with fertilisers and manures is not always appreciated by native plants.

* Claire fertilises at the time of planting with a pinch of native plant formula at the base of the hole. She waters the plants in, and nurses them for the first summer. This means watering once or twice a week in hot weather with a drip irrigation system. 'Gardening in deep Western Australian sand is rather like hydroponics,' she says, 'so about once a year during the main growing season, I give some of the plants more fertiliser.'

Architect of light

Howard Tanner has a reputation for a love of heritage. As a thoroughly modern architect, Howard is not keen on the 'heritage architect' label, however. His design briefs include an eclectic range of new projects, where 'clients appreciate what you are doing and want to build properly'.

In the spirit of nineteenth century English architect Edwin Lutyens, and Australian Professor Leslie Wilkinson, Howard takes a keen interest in the connection between house and garden in his residential projects. 'It's impossible for me not to consider both,' he says.

For Howard, the arrangement of terraces and courtyards provide a platform for the house. He is often asked to provide a strong landscape master plan, showing the expanses of lawn and placement of main trees.

'I expect the owners or the plantsman they hire to bring in wonderful planted detail—but it must be detail that will thrive in the climate.

'The thing about gardens,' says Howard, 'is that they have a mind of their own. If you plant unwisely in Sydney, for instance, the plants will soon decide what to do.' He acknowledges that Sydney is a difficult gardening climate. 'It's neither the tulips of the Southern Highlands, nor the roses of South Australia, and it's not truly sub-tropical. The joy here in winter is the camellia. Then you have the gordonias, followed by *Magnolia denudata*, with its wonderful honey-lemon scent.'

Howard believes that Sydney's native trees are under-used. 'I think a stand of angophora in the right rocky setting can be wonderful. The lilly pilly grows marvellously on the harbour foreshore, either as hedges or a well-formed tree.'

He cites the tough Queenslanders, such as *Ficus hillii*, as suited to the Sydney climate. He loves the beautifully scented climber *Stephanotis*, as well as the old fashioned, pastel-toned *Hibiscus syriacus*. Lemon trees and gardenias are also favourites. 'You are trying to build up a language,' says Howard, who includes South African bulbs such as ixias and freesias in his vocabulary.

His own garden combines strong design elements with favourite plants. A large room opens on one side to a big terrace which is elevated above the street, and which affords views to the Blue Mountains. Slide back the doors on the other side and you reveal a sheltered garden; banks of camellia and magnolia create privacy.

Howard extolls the joys of living on the verandah. 'In Sydney you must extend the house into the garden. In the 1920s the biggest room in the house was an expansive north-facing verandah with settees and a canvas drop to keep out the worst weather.

'The grander the view the simpler the garden,' says Howard. 'I think if a client wanted a very fussy garden I would encourage them to focus on, say, one detailed border—and one must not be too complicated on a small site.

'It's very good to have a few intrigues. You can think "Oh, there's a path; there's another garden area down there." Even on the tightest city block one longs for interludes.

'It's the oblique incidence that often sticks in the mind. I remember going to a Wilkinson house, years ago. It didn't look much from outside, but once inside, the whole house stretched away from the street, facing a sunny northern garden. Wilkinson understood the nuances of sunlight, outlook and privacy,' explains Howard. 'He advised "Aspect not prospect".'

Opposite: *Magnolia stellata* 'Rosea'.

Below: *Stephanotis floribunda*.

Bottom left: *Magnolia* x *soulangeana*

How this garden works

* Howard Tanner agrees that the garden must complement the house. 'You can decide that there are one or two elements that might have been typical. In Edwardian times, for instance, there would have been a big jacaranda.'

* 'In modern city gardens you must be very careful about the scale of trees,' he says.

* In warmer climates camellias do well in a south-facing garden, where they won't discolour in the sun.

* In Howard Tanner's Sydney garden, Vireya rhododendron grow well in pots.

Winter

Favourite trees

Gardeners, usually obsessive and sometimes greedy, can never decide when to stop. There is always just one more treasure they can't resist. If you had room for only one last tree and wanted something special, what would you choose?

Certain trees seem to convey the Australian spirit. You can't imagine the river red gum (*Eucalyptus camaldulensis*) in any other setting but the Australian countryside. The sight of the massive trunks and outstretched arms evokes the greys and mist-blues of a Hans Heysen painting that captures so immediately the essence of Australian beauty.

If autumn is the time for a foliage fireworks display, it is in winter that the wonderful bark of many trees is most obvious. The twisted trunks of the high country snow gums display a wide palette of colours at any time of the year, but are even more startling in winter when the early setting sun lights the swirls of pinks, greens and yellows against a canvas of snow.

Some of the maples have extraordinary bark; *Acer griseum*, the paperbark maple, develops its splendid trunk of pink, papery bark at a very early age. In winter the red trunks of *Acer palmatum* 'Senkaki' seem to take on an even more brilliant sheen.

One of the trees most sought after for its bark is *Betula albo-sinensis* with its peeling, pink and crimson bark. This medium-sized tree is best planted in groups or copses where the limbs will soon 'hold hands'.

The designer Kath Carr used to talk about 'ballerina arms'; she loved *Prunus mume* and the *Malus floribunda* for their graceful arms and would weigh down new limbs with twine and a stone to gently encourage horizontal lines. *Cornus controversa* 'Variegata' is loved for its elegant horizontal arrangement of branches.

It pays to research carefully your choice. Many an evergreen alder (*Alnus acuminata*) has had to be removed from a city garden after becoming popular in the late 1980s as the perfect tree for a small garden. Incredibly fast growing, happily reaching a height of 15 metres, in Sydney this alder was soon pushing over fences. Another quick grower, if you have the room, is *Zelkova serrata*. In the same family as the elm, this tree has the added advantage of flaking bark and leaves that turn bronze or red in autumn.

Nothing looks sadder than a tree that has outgrown the space available, and had its lower limbs removed or its branches chopped off at the elbow, perhaps to allow for the easy access of the mower.

Tree surgeon and arborist Alex Bicknell recommends that home gardeners 'leave well alone. It's a common misconception that if you remove the lower branches the tree will grow faster,' he says. 'In fact the reverse is true. Low branches are very important to shade the trunk and the root area, and when a tree is small they might amount to 30 per cent of the leaf area, thus they are feeding the tree.

'If you skin the trunk, the tree is going to slow down. With trees like golden cypress, oaks and elms, removing low branches is the beginning of a cycle of collapse which continues throughout the life of the tree, because the branch above grows into the space created, becomes heavier than it should, and will eventually collapse, and so on, toward the tree's inevitable decline.'

Bicknell adds that low branches will die naturally when their use to the tree is complete. 'And a tree growing naturally, with low branches sweeping the ground, will never suffer a break in the crown,' he says.

Opposite left: *Betula albo-sinensis*.

Opposite right: The leopard tree, *Caesalpinia ferrea*.

Below: *Eucalyptus camaldulensis*.

Bottom left: *Arbutus unedo*.

How this garden works

* As the young stems are a brilliant red, some gardeners annually coppice *Acer palmatum* 'Senkaki' to encourage new growth.

* Alex Bicknell emphasises the importance of ensuring against a sharp fork forming in a growing tree. 'It's a badly formed main fork if the angle resembles a V; this may eventually break. A fork resembling a U will be strong.'

* Weigh down new limbs to prevent converging trunks.

Hedges

There is no time like winter for making tough decisions in the garden. Without their costume of green, gold or bronze finery, the bones of the winter garden are laid bare for contemplation and scrutiny. Winter is the time when one's creative shortcomings are all too obvious, but it's also the time of great satisfaction as design mistakes are rectified. The winter garden is anything but dull, particularly if hedges have been used to create the basis of the garden over which the planting detail is laid.

Hedges divide the garden into manageable sections; they contain the different planting schemes and moods, they edge and define, and direct the garden visitor along discretely planned garden routes.

At Al Ru Farm in South Australia, Ruth Irving has very definite ideas on hedging. 'Box hedges are restrained; you are putting in the bones of the garden, so scale and quality is crucial,' she says. 'Hedges should be slow to medium growing, not a mile a minute. You don't want too much maintenance.'

In the Southern Highlands of New South Wales, Hillview, the fascinating garden of plantsman Dean Havelberg, is designed around circles and curves of clipped box. Several severely clipped cones add drama and connect the various components, while pyramids of variegated box (*Buxus sempervirens* 'Variegata') are used to brighten certain parts of the garden.

At Cloudehill in Victoria's Dandenongs, Jeremy Francis uses hedges of hornbeam, beech, rhododendron and cedar (*Thuja* spp.), to create structure in a large garden. A favourite plant for hedging is the hornbeam (*Carpinus betulus*). 'It gives the impression of beech but is much easier.' he says.

that hang on for weeks over autumn. Pruning the rugosas with a chain-saw is a myth, however; the teeth of the chainsaw catch in the thorny branches and do untold damage.

At Joan Arnold's Busker's End, the low growing *Pittosporum* 'Tom Thumb' makes an unusual hedge, its cerise colour adding drama through the year. Here it restrains a mass planting of red tulips which are backed with a hedge of *Viburnum* x *juddii*; its crimson buds open to the palest pink flowers and have a marvellous fragrance. In this garden, hedges are also used to support all manner of climbers, so that interest and excitement continue through the seasons.

At Benara Homestead in South Australia, the magnificent hedges, which are more then 100 years old, have to be seen to be believed.

Opposite: Cypress hedges at Benara are more than 100 years old.

Left: Turrets and cylinders: clipped hedges at Benara Homestead, Mount Gambier.

Rob Cowell has recently restored a collection of beautiful nineteenth century stone buildings at his Black Springs Bakery, near Beechworth in northern Victoria. Hedges are of myrtle (*Luma apiculata*), which Rob believes is better than the more traditional box. 'It's faster growing, has scented white flowers and good foliage,' he says. There are hedges of lavender also, which thrive in the dry climate. In misty mountain climates, the Russian sage, *Perovskia atriplicifolia*, is more successful. Ruth Irving uses the greys and blues of the catmint, *Nepeta* x *faassenii*, for hedging and to tie the various parts of the garden together.

For seaside gardens the coast daisy (*Olearia axelaris*) performs well, as does the versatile *Correa reflexa*, the tea-tree, *Melaleuca lanceolata*, and the sea box, *Alyxia buxifolia*, which, in a maritime environment, may be preferable to English box. The white flowered *Escallonia* 'Iveyi' makes a fast growing hedge which clips well; it will create a microclimate to protect treasures from salt laden winds.

The rugosa species of roses make strong and beautiful informal hedges; my current favourite is either *Rosa rugosa alba* with its large, white, fragile-looking flowers, or *R. r.* 'Agnes', with its soft yellow double blooms. Rugosa roses, in my experience, need no watering, no fertilising and reward one with constant blossom over summer and brilliant hips

How this garden works

* At Hillview, hedges are clipped just after spring, once the new leaves emerge. A light 'haircut' is given in mid summer to keep the plantings dense.

* *Westringia fruticosa* makes a successful hedge in a dry climate, but requires clipping from an early age if it is to become thick from the base. *Teucrium fruticans* is another grey-leaved plant which makes a great hedge, with regular clipping.

* Prune a may hedge (*Spiraea* spp.), and other plants which grow in long canes, from the base, cutting out a few canes at a time, allowing the plant to maintain its natural form and avoiding a woeful truncated appearance.

* If you like pruning, tapestry hedges are an exciting alternative to fencing. Try beech and maple for autumn colour, the hawthorns for berries, and the different hollies and pittosporums for leaf cover in winter. At Wombat Park in Victoria, hedges are clipped regularly. 'Once you get the shape you want, stick to that line. The hedge will gradually thicken down to the ground,' says gardener, Stewart Henderson.

Impossible choice

In many parts of Australia, the last rose blooms linger as many gardeners procrastinate over pruning. Many more are pouring over rose catalogues from specialist growers, wondering where in their garden they could possibly fit another plant. It's hard to resist those catalogues; 'just a quick look' is fatal. There will always be something you must have, and it won't be worth ordering just one or two—for it's impossible to discriminate with roses. Ask any rose lover, 'What's your favourite rose?' and they'll answer, 'The one I saw yesterday.'

So, which rose is the best and fairest? Is it 'Ophelia', with her perfect blooms, her delicate, crushed-silk colour and her exquisite scent? Is it her offspring, the Hybrid Musk 'Penelope', who looks unbeatable grown as a loose hedge with her cousins, the peachy 'Cornelia', 'Felicia' and even 'Gruss an Aachen'? The small-flowered 'Green Ice' also looks great with the scrambling, groundcovering 'Heidesommer'; backed with a hedge of box, it's desperately smart.

Another absolute must (isn't gardening like this—there are so many treasures one simply *must* have, but must *not*?) is a hedge of the rose *rugosa alba*. Her deep green glossy leaves are in perfect counterpoint to her abundant, large white flowers which are followed by red hips—which make great jelly, if you are into making lots of work for yourself.

Surely the most beautiful rose is 'Devoniensis', clotted cream in colour and so generous in her flowering. She would look marvellous

planted with those other rich-cream climbers, 'Sombreuil' and 'Lamarque'. Rather than being boring because of their similarity, the slight difference in form and flower shape would add layer upon delicious layer of enchantment. Or is it the 100-year-old cream-with-pink rose growing over a tennis court on an old property in South Australia's Clare Valley? She's a must, but no expert can confirm her name. She's similar to 'Marie van Houtte', but thicker, richer—with a scent that makes you constantly sigh, 'Ah, now that's a rose.'

Is it 'Mme Gregoire Stacehlin'? She's a pink rose, but she's not just any pink rose. Her semi-double, snooty flowers are followed by golden hips. She looks fabulous with *Clematis texensis* 'Gravetye Beauty' covering her bare legs. The clematis flowers cerise, all summer long; as the rosehips are forming so are the marvellous yellow seed heads of the clematis. Mad.

'New Dawn' is a constantly-flowering, shell-pink climber which tones perfectly with *Teucrium fruticans*. She's divine scrambling through an informal hedge of the grey-leaved teucrium; she's easy to propagate from cuttings and, with the copper-pink 'Albertine' (brutal thorns and only spring-flowering), will cover a country fence and give you endless, delicate colour. 'Blossomtime' is great in this company too, and has perhaps the most beautiful buds—long, elegant and suffused with carmine.

'Souvenir de la Malmaison', named for Napoleon's Josephine, is divine when she's behaving herself. If you can't cope with her tantrums, try 'Pierre de Ronsard', bred by the Meilland family, who brought the world the 'Peace' rose. She's voluptuous but never big and blowsy—

white, edged with candy pink, she blooms for months, until just after Easter. With the once-only 'Constance Spry' and the climbing peppermint geranium (which will strike from a cutting), she will quickly cover an old shed.

The 'old fashioneds' are subtle, but just as beautiful if you take the time and trouble to look. While many are thorny, they team well with vegetables in 'the potager'—and make delicious tea, and cake flavourings, if you resist the sprays. The almost-thornless 'Duchesse de Buccleugh' with her sweet face, is the epitomy of restraint and good breeding.

Old-rose aficionados will eschew the David Austin roses, bred by the Englishman for old fashioned form and scent, but modern remontancy. They are justly popular, however—full, luscious, in a range of beautiful colours and mostly wonderfully scented. The best is, perhaps, the new 'Glamis Castle'—again that rich cream colour. Or is it 'Sweet Juliet', with endless apricot-coloured flowers toning perfectly with mass plantings of iris, dianthus and stachys?

The deep-red David Austins such as 'Othello' have a scent reminiscent of the old Bourbon 'Mme Isaac Pereire', which many will name as their favourite. Oh, let's forget restraint and discipline, and have them all.

Opposite: Roses 'Albertine' and 'Wedding Day' cover old wooden stables.

Left: 'Wedding Day' with 'Albertine' are prominent in Warwick Vyner's garden.

Below: The exquisite 'Albertine' rose.

Winter cheer

Joan Arnold's renowned garden, Busker's End, in the Southern Highlands of New South Wales, has one, trained around a pillar at the end of a vista; at the Matcham Valley Plant Place on the Central Coast 'Dixie Knight Supreme' is the colour of thick cream, splashed with the red of strawberry jam; at Don Burke's mountain garden the new 'Marj Millar' cascades down a bank as a very successful groundcover, and at the Cassidy garden near Bright in north-east Victoria, the collection is extensive and erudite. They flower from Easter, and will cheer short winter days, until September, when our interest is stolen by so much, so suddenly, in the garden. They are, of course, camellias.

Peg and Harry Cassidy's 0.5 hectare garden at Harrietville is home to over 200 camellias. The Cassidys are members of several plant societies which allows them to indulge in their passion for collecting, particularly of camellias and rhododendron. Among the *Camellia* is one of the Higo form, *C. japonica* 'Yamato Nishiki', which has pink, white and marbled flowers on the same plant. There is *C. japonica* 'Madame de Saumarez' growing on the same plant as the fringed-petalled 'Fred Sander'; there is *C. reticulata* 'Crimson Robe'. The high-altitude garden, also home to a collection of rare conifers, is dominated by the sounds of the Ovens River, which rushes along the boundary, augmented in spring by the melting snow from the surrounding mountains.

Busker's End, the Bowral garden of plantswoman Joan Arnold, is fascinating at any time of the year. From early autumn, sheets of *Cyclamen hederifolium* cover the ground; then a deep red carpet of liquidambar leaves is brightened with emerging snow-white *Helleborus niger*. Interest is extended throughout winter by clever use of the viburnums, planted for autumn colour and winter flowers and berries. There is *Viburnum farreri* and its cultivars as well as the gloriously scented *V. carlesii* and *V.* x *bodnantense*. Mahonias, some of which are perfumed, after bursting into plumes of yellow flowers are followed by purple fruit. In winter, the skimmias are a mass of berries.

At Busker's End, camellias are often used as support plants. 'In early summer the big flowers of the 'Jackmanii' clematis, twining against the camellia's dark green, glossy foliage, look fabulous,' says Joan. 'The hybrid fuchsia likes the same conditions as the camellias; their wandy growth twisted through the camellia looks out of this world. If you live in a cold climate, grow the flame-red climbing nasturtium (*Tropaeolum speciosum*) through camellias; in England it grows through a yew hedge.

If you don't like the bright red, grow the climbing *Dicentra scandens*, which has a yellow flower.'

Joan likes camellias to be grown in an area of their own, and does not mix japonicas with sasanquas. 'They are not the same in form and shape,' she says. 'You can use japonica cultivars to extend the flowering season. The *Camellia* x *williamsii* cultivars are particularly long-flowering in a colder climate. 'Donation', 'Anticipation' and 'E. G. Waterhouse' are lovely.'

At Busker's End, the long whippy branches of the *sasanqua* camellia 'Mine-no-yuki' are twisted to cover a pillar to draw the eye to the conclusion of a vista. Elsewhere, it is woven into itself to make a hedge.

Opposite: Winter at Busker's End.

Below: The January border at Busker's End.

Camellias

Flowering in Australia from early winter until spring, the camellia has been in cultivation in China at least since 500 BC. Its seeds are prized for oil for cosmetics, the leaves for tea, and the flowers as symbols of refinement and beauty.

Camellias have always inspired artists, from creators of the delicate silk and china paintings of the Orient, to our own botanical artists determined to capture both the strength and the luminescence of their petals. *Camellia japonica* 'Nuccio's Gem' must surely be the camellia that inspired many a Paul Jones watercolour; the flower is formal, its petals perfectly imbricated, its texture like the complexion of some renowned beauty in literature. It is the ultimate flower for the lapel or evening shirt.

Camellias do well in most parts of Australia, even in the tricky Sydney climate. They are particularly useful in small city gardens where they will allow themselves to be clipped and twisted to espalier along lateral wires on a city paling fence. *Camellia sasanqua* 'Setsugekka' with its masses of fluted white flowers on long and subtle limbs, is particularly successful; prune after flowering, to train new growth along the wires.

The Australian-bred *Camellia japonica* 'Brushfield's Yellow' will form a great hedge, its yellow flowers lighting up wintery skies. (This camellia lines the drive to Japan's Imperial Palace.) The variegated leaves of the *Camellia japonica* 'Benten' will also light up a dark area in the garden.

It was of course the plant hunters of the last century who brought the world these plants, collecting seeds and specimens in wild and dangerous country. The most intrepid, and the most successful, must have been George Forrest who, in July 1905, had based himself at the French Catholic Mission at Tzekou, 3000 metres up in Yunnan province at the point where China, India and Tibet meet. He escaped death at the hands of furious Tibetan lamas only through feats of daring, ingenuity and determination, such that make those of Indiana Jones look pedestrian. As he finally escaped, climbing to 7000 metres in mountainous Yunnan, he could still record, 'Up and up we climbed, cutting our way through miles of rhododendrons, tramping over alps literally clothed with primulas, gentians, saxifrages, lilies etc., for these unknown hillsides are a veritable botanists' paradise'. Plant lovers today will sympathise with such passion.

Left: *Camellia sasanqua* 'Setsugekka'.

How this garden works

* 'Camellias enjoy a soil range from neutral to acid,' says Joan Arnold. 'Clematis need a cool root run; plant just outside the roots of the camellia to allow growth towards the sun.'

* Because of the difference in form, shape and growing habit it is best not to mix the various species of camellia. Joan Arnold recommends using *Camellia japonica* cultivars to extend the flowering season. Use *Camellia* x *williamsii* cultivars, such as the large-flowered, pink, 'Donation', in a colder climate.

* Don't espalier camellias on a new wall; the lime in the render or point work is not to the liking of these acid-loving plants.

* The camellia is named in honour of the Jesuit, Georg Josef Kamel, who worked in the Philippines early in the eighteenth century.

Australia's natural wonder

At the foot of Canberra's Black Mountain is the Australian National Botanic Garden, a 40-hectare garden of Australian native plants, started in 1949. The Garden was extensively developed in the 1960s and 1970s by its first curator, John Wrigley, whose work with the Society for Growing Australian Plants was well known. He had also been instrumental in the creation of Sydney's Ku-ring-gai Wildflower Garden.

The major themes throughout the garden are either ecological or taxonomic, and the collection of over 5500 species represents nearly one third of Australia's known flora. 'This is a true botanic garden, combining science, education and conservation with a good design,' says curator, horticulturalist Leslie Lockwood.

The Garden is a research institution and, with the CSIRO, runs the Centre for Plant Biodiversity Research. Plantings throughout the Garden are informal, emphasising the unique qualities of Australia's indigenous plants from the various plant communities throughout the country.

One of the several exciting areas is the rainforest gully, displaying many Australian rainforest communities. As the visitor climbs up, through the rainforest gully, he transects the east coast of Australia, moving from the cool-climate rainforest of Tasmania in the lower part, on to the cool Gippsland rainforest and then to northern Australian tropical rainforest communities as he reaches the head of the gully. While the cooler areas of Queensland, such as the Atherton Tableland and Mount Bellinden Ker can drop to just 1°C at night, growing the coastal rainforest of tropical Queensland is a challenge in the Canberra climate. A glasshouse at the top of the gully is definitely on the wish list!

The 'Sydney Flora area' is a new project which displays the diverse flora of Sydney's Hawkesbury sandstone, from the flannel flower to Sydney's range of pea flowers. There is also a eucalypt lawn of over 100 species throughout a carefully maintained lawn of several hectares.

Marked trails take the visitor through the different areas, including the Rock Garden and the Mallee Shrublands; there are also guided tours each day at 11.00 a.m., and also at 2.00 p.m. on weekends.

Above: *Acacia decurrens* in bloom.

Racecourse Inn

Mid winter is the time to stock up on gardening books, brochures and catalogues, settle down in front of the fire and dream of grand garden plans. You learn the most by looking at the best, and there is no better way to learn about garden design than to look at our greatest gardens. Cold and wet weather is the perfect excuse to extend yourself no further than planning garden visits for spring and summer.

Tasmania is excessively beautiful—almost too beautiful. It takes your breath away. Spring and summer arrive slowly and hedgerows of hawthorn which are 'lain down' in the English tradition, and which dissect emerald-green fields, are covered in pink and white confetti in late November. White settlement dates from 1803, when 49 people, including 24 convicts, arrived at Risdon Cove, close to the present-day Hobart. Today, Georgian buildings glow in a mellow, late afternoon light; road edges, bridges and walls are convict-built, of sandstone.

As you might expect, Tasmania is also a state of glorious gardens, many of which you can visit and within which you can stay. Many grand houses and gardens were designed as new settlers sought to re-create the picturesque landscapes of 'home', depicted by colonial artists and discussed by the influential nineteenth century English garden writers such as John Claudius Loudon. Tasmania's gardens house

Garden lovers can stay at the Racecourse Inn, enjoying Robyn's delicious home cooking, much of which is created from the produce of her large vegetable garden—which is also greatly appreciated by her chooks. Robyn's orchard, boasting seven types of plum, as well as crabapples, plump apricots, cherries and white peaches, dates to the property's establishment and provides guests' breakfast tables with 17 different preserves.

A 0.5 hectare, rambling, cottage-style garden surrounds the Inn. To the south of the house is a shaded garden of rhododendron and camellias, foxgloves, hellebores and hostas, protected from the road by a high hedge of hawthorn which is pruned twice a year. The yellow rose 'Gold Bunny', covering a side wall of convict-made brick, flowers in early November, while outbuildings are smothered with the thornless apricot-coloured 'Crepuscule' and the gold tea rose 'Lady Hillingdon'. In December, swathes of poppies along the front of the Inn, which is listed by the National Trust, are a traffic-stopping sight.

The Behind the Hedges Garden Tours leave from here, and visit eight of the outstanding private gardens in the area, including Annabel Scott's Dunedin, a plantlover's paradise and Panshanger, a large garden set around one of Australia's most beautiful Regency houses.

A 1998/99 addition to the tour is Belmont, built in 1823 by John Pascoe Fawkner who came to Australia in 1803, accompanying his convict father. Belmont is a garden 'in reconstruction'—yet another example of the cornucopia of horticultural, heritage and culinary treats that awaits the traveller in Tasmania.

Opposite: Racecourse Inn, built in 1840.

Left: 'Gold Bunny' blooms during November.

magnificent trees, some planted as seed brought from England in ancestral pockets in the 1820s.

Robyn and Bill Baker run their perfectly organised Behind the Hedges Garden Tours from their historic Racecourse Inn, which was built in 1840 as a coaching house for travellers through Tasmania's beautiful Midlands en route from Hobart to Launceston. The Racecourse Inn is at Longford, a charming town of antique shops and original buildings—and the oldest continuously operating racecourse in Australia, dating from 1846. Longford, surveyed in 1813, is today 15 minutes from Launceston—and is the setting for many inspirational gardens.

How this garden works

* At the Racecourse Inn, fruit trees are pruned religiously in July, and sprayed with a Bordeaux mixture. Bill Baker always sprays late in the day, after the bees have gone to bed. He only uses non toxic preparations, including pyrethrums and white oil.

* The traditional hedging method of 'laying down' involves cutting the hedge almost through, at its base. The hedge is then lain on its side, from where it re-grows, creating a barrier, impenetrable to cattle.

Ruth Leitch

Ruth Leitch lives in the most difficult gardening country imaginable. Summers can be searing, the rainfall of some 500 millimetres per year is irregular, and there is clay under a thin layer of black soil. Not only does Ruth garden, however, but her 1.5-hectare garden, Combadello, west of Moree in northern New South Wales, is serene and beautiful, due to good management and appropriate planting.

'The rainfall is 20 inches, which may not be too bad, but we can get 7 inches in one day,' says Ruth, 'The 1990s have been 10 drought years, and here I have no underground water. The first thing I did when I came here in 1951 was build up the beds and add mulch—and we kept adding.'

With summers over 40°C (and at night the temperature drops only a few degrees) the verandahs and the double bull-nose around the house, built in 1887, are design essentials.

Perhaps the most dramatic feature of Combadello is its entrance. You arrive at the garden, which is set within a wheat station, to find a semi-circle of cottonwoods (*Populus deltoides*) protecting the house. A walkway of six, 100-year-old Canary Island palms leads to the house, and provides the main axis between the house and garden. 'Those trees create the atmosphere of this garden, as well as wonderful shade,' says Ruth.

Throughout the garden are special trees such as *Celtis australis*—a shade tree greatly loved by the birds. 'Its new, broad, lime-green leaves in spring, after pretty bitter winters, are very welcome,' says Ruth, 'and it has a wonderful shape and form.' Ruth adds that one of the best trees for the area is the white cedar, which will 'survive anything'.

'In summer it's hard to get anything to survive,' she says. 'Agapanthus, iris and lilies do well and the osteospermums self-sow.' At Combadello, great use is made of sedums and of euphorbias. 'I love the contrast of colours—the lime-green contrasts with spring pinks and yellows.'

Throughout the garden, the greys of dianthus mix with cream and pale pink ranunculus and massed white daisies and pelargoniums. The wrong colour often pops up and is left, Ruth accedes. Combadello is mainly a spring garden because of the extreme summers, when water is sacrificed to keep the cooling lawn looking good.

A central feature of the garden is the natural lagoon, which is home to a teeming birdlife—ibis, pelicans and water hens.

'I created the garden around the house and for the children,' says Ruth Leitch today. 'There are little spots with special meaning—places to sit with children and grandchildren.'

Left: Combadello's impressive garden.

How this garden works

* At Combadello, Ruth Leitch has planted flame trees, kurrajongs and that Edna Walling favourite, the mugga ironbark, *Sideroxylon rosea*, with its glaucous leaves and furrowed, black bark—all do well without too much water.

Ditchfield

itchfield, near Moss Vale in the Southern Highlands of New South Wales, has been created over nine years by designer and nurseryman, Geoff Duxfield and his wife Chris Hurditch, a florist. The garden must survive tough conditions; while the rainfall is almost 1000 millilitres (40 inches) a year, the garden has to cope with heavy, and late, frosts. Geoff believes in making his plants work for their living and in not pampering plants—'so they can cope with a dry spell when necessary'.

You enter the garden by a grey-painted wooden gate and a long and winding drive. At the end of the drive a hedge of *Hebe* provides colour in winter as well as protection from winds.

Some of the most successful plants in this garden are the cistus, the statuesque echiums, the grey-leaved santolinas and lavenders, and the blue-flowered ceanothus and teucrium which have all starred in the recent drought. One of the hardest working plants at Ditchfield is the generous *Cerinthe major* 'Purpurea', a self-seeding annual, which happily fills in the borders each year.

Geoff is particularly interesting on the subject of the versatile, winter-flowering woodspurge, the *Euphorbia* species. 'They are tough and almost maintenance free,' he says. 'And the yellow flowers are welcome in the coldest months when flowers are scarce.'

Euphorbias make very good cut flowers, although the sap is poisonous. *Euphorbia amygdaloides* grows in moist, shaded, woodland areas in Yugoslavia and Portugal. *Euphorbia characias* subsp. *wulfenii*, with its blue-green leaves and acid-green flower heads, is a high country plant. It is frost hardy and will thrive in terrible conditions, although it will grow in Sydney if given good drainage. In Beth Chatto's garden in a very dry part of England, her plantings of bright pink poppies with this euphorbia are much admired. At Ditchfield, *E. characias* subsp. *characias* has self-seeded in the gravel, along with *Echium wildpretii*, a biennial with spires of pink flowers.

'*E. myrsinites* is a great plant and will grow in gravel with no water. It's great for trailling over walls,' says Geoff. In his garden, it grows in gravel by the front door with *E. rigida*, a native of Iran. The combination looks most effective, backed by a hedge of the grey-leaved *Teucrium fruticans*. These two euphorbias grow well in pots, requiring almost no water.

Geoff runs a wholesale nursery specialising in hardy and cold-

climate plants. 'Echiums are a fantastic plant, if you can give them protection in a cold climate by growing them around the house,' says Geoff. 'They are quick growing, great for adding structure, and absolutely spectacular when in flower.'

Echium candicans (or *fastuosum*) comes in several forms, including a variety developed by Duxfield called 'Ditchfield Blue'.

Above: *Euphorbia myrsinites.*

How this garden works

* Geoff Duxfield starts a new garden bed by hoeing the area first, then laying down newspaper, followed by mushroom compost, and then spoiled lucerne hay. This mulch saves water and restricts weeds. It also provides an even ground temperature, particularly preventing vegetables from becoming too hot in summer.

* At Ditchfield the vegetable garden is given a prized position in front of the house—not tucked away, out of sight—prompting constant maintenance and use!

Fallen leaves

Just an hour from Melbourne are the Macedon Ranges, home to many well established, cold-climate, 'hill station' gardens. At an altitude of 1064 metres, the gardens of Mount Macedon, perhaps the best known of the villages of the area, are a mecca for garden lovers. The National Trust has stated that the Mount Macedon gardens 'represent one of the most important collections of nineteenth century gardens in Australia. Their importance is not so much in the individual design of each garden but rather as a collection. Botanically and horticulturally the gardens are also of importance and ... reflect the prevailing social attitudes and aspirations of the late nineteenth century.' One of several such gardens is Alton, now undergoing major restoration under new owners, Marj and Ed Eshuys.

Alton was built in 1875 for Sir George Verdon, a politician, barrister and banker; in 1860, at the age of 26, he was the Victorian treasurer. The entry for Verdon in the Australian Dictionary of Biography describes Alton as a 'handsome summer mansion'.

Verdon was a trustee of the arts, president of the National Gallery from 1883 to 1896, president of the Victorian Institute of Architects and a patron of the government astronomer, who owned the neighbouring property, Hascombe, also an important garden. Verdon was also a colleague of Baron Ferdinand Von Mueller, who was the first director of Melbourne's Botanic Gardens, and who assisted Verdon in his collection of exotic trees. Part of the conditions of acquiring land in the area was that at least 10 forest trees had to be planted, and when Verdon died in 1896, he left a valuable arboretum of some 18 acres (8 hectares).

The property was eventually bought, in 1926, by George Nicholas of *Aspro* fame. Nicholas terraced the steeply sloping site to reduce water loss and constructed the tennis court, which is set dramatically into the hillside. His extensive program of planting saw mature trees being brought from England and transported to the top of the mountain by horse-drawn wagon. It was Nicholas who added the retaining walls, the stone paths and flights of massive steps which are so crucial to the structure and the character of the garden today.

Fortunately, the garden suffered only minor damage in the bushfires of 1983, when so many important gardens were lost; today, Alton is said to have the best private collection of large conifers in Victoria.

A weeping beech (*Fagus sylvatica* 'Pendula') is just one of several outstanding trees in the garden. There is also a massive Himalayan cedar, a Californian redwood, a Spanish chestnut, and several larch. The terraced mountain garden is full of reds and golds in autumn; in winter the leaf-litter-rich soil is a mass of emerging spring bulbs, and in summer collections of hydrangea come into their own.

'There are so many joys in a garden like Alton,' says Marj Eshuys. 'There is its historical significance, the grandeur of the old trees, the challenge of restoration to recapture some of its original splendour—and there's the joy of sharing it with others.'

Opposite: Secret paths wind through this mountain garden.

Left: Stonework forms strong bones throughout the garden.

Below: An ochre carpet of fallen leaves in early winter at Alton.

Winter dreaming

The gardener's life is one of constant adventure, as each new month introduces excitement, and enchantment. Winter is never a sad time when you're a gardener, as the blue-green tips of spring bulbs burst through frozen soil, promising so much. Excitement mounts as spring approaches, as swelling leaf-buds on winter-bare trees assure you that the seasons will go, indeed, the full circle.

Yet many gardens are still in winter's steely grip. There are those glorious clear, sunny days of mid winter, but there are plenty of days that provide the perfect excuse for putting on the kettle and garden-dreaming. The balmy days of late August will then arrive, and you'll be fooled into thinking that winter is over—but you'll soon find that packing away the winter paraphernalia is premature and early morning frosts will again bring their special delight.

Winter is the time tiny treasures emerge, all the more precious as colour is so scarce. It takes time and trouble to notice some of this season's special offerings, such as the true snowdrop, *Galanthus* spp. These delicate and shy bulbs are slow to multiply, and not as economic as the easier *Leucojum*, the common snowflake. It may be only you who notices them hiding among fallen leaves and winter grasses, but the exquisite markings of the true snowdrop make them very collectable. Photographing them is like reaching into their soul; you understand their integrity and can sympathise with cultures who abhor having their spirit captured on film.

The hardy winter rose, *Helleborus* spp.—commonly called the Christmas rose in England, for obvious reasons—carpets the ground throughout the chilly season. You could be forgiven for thinking she is rather plain—until you look carefully into her face, which is full of

Soon spring will come, however, with new treats such as the fritillaries. And if you covet those meadows in England where the chequerboard snake's head *Fritillaria meleagris* and black tulips seem to grow like weeds, take heart—it is not effortless. In Wiltshire, a full-time guard is assigned to look after the health and safety of the meadow near the village of Cricklade, as garden tourists emerge from winter hibernation to marvel at the new season's offerings.

Opposite left: *Helleborus lividus* in the chill of a winter's morning.

Opposite right: *Magnolia denudata* sparkles when covered with frost.

Left: *Helleborus lividus*

Below: *Helleborus* 'Mrs Betty Ranicar'.

character. There is nothing ordinary about *Helleborus orientalis* with her flowers of exquisite colours and markings. One coveted form is *H.* 'Mrs Betty Ranicar', a double white, named after a much-loved Tasmanian gardener. *H. lividus* is a species of handsome foliage and illuminated green flowers. All are perfect for filling out a perennial border when plants less brave have retreated underground.

Winter is also the time for the magnolia, when frosted buds give way to showy scented branches. Now is arguably the time to cut out crossing branches—the only pruning the magnolia should need—to enjoy extravagant indoor flower arrangements for which decorators might stage midnight garden raids. The magnolias start flowering in the darkest days of winter with the dreamy, white, lemon-scented *M. denudata*; then comes the delicate *M.* x *loebneri* 'Margaret Merrill' to be followed by *M. stellata*, finishing with the justifiably ever-popular, French-bred *M.* x *soulangeana*.

Freesias thrive even in sandy Sydney—in fact they hate the frost of colder climates. The old fashioned *Freesia alba* is deliciously scented, while the florist-bought forced blooms smell of salt and pepper. Winter is a time when we welcome yellow in the garden, admire the bigger splashes of daffodils—easy going and simple pleasures to fill the house with golden light.

How this garden works

* *Helleborus niger* is one of the most exciting of the hellebores—cut off the leaves at summer's end so that the startling white flowers emerge like fallen snow on fallen autumn leaves. Divide hellebores after flowering. Cut down the leaves to make lifting out of the ground with a spade easier. Turn the clump over and cut through into several pieces with a sharp knife.

* Magnolias love moisture retaining, slightly acidic soil, although *M.* x *soulangeana* will tolerate a wider range of soils. Mulch annually with aged manure. Prune (usually after flowering) only to remove crossing branches; much of the charm of the magnolia is its relaxed, spreading, multi-stemmed form.

Mount George

The diverse climate of South Australia's Adelaide Hills has resulted in an extraordinary range of gardens to provide continuous fascination for the horticulturalist. There are the cool climate gardens of exotic plantings that provide a fabulous display of autumn colour and winter structure. There are the gardens of plantsmen and women who, mindful of the dry summers, plant for winter thrills. There are winery gardens which look to Mediterranean and Provençal traditions in their choice of plantings, while the turning vines provide a golden patchwork in April. The mood of the Adelaide Hills changes, therefore, almost at every turn.

When Bob and Betty Lewis bought their property, Mount George, some 30 years ago, they inherited a terraced garden of cold climate trees set in the midst of mountains clothed in the candlebark gum, *Eucalyptus viminalis* and *E. rubida*, as well as, higher up, stringybarks, *E. obliqua*.

The property was taken up by Abraham Ashhurst and his family, who were given a lease of crown land by Queen Victoria in 1851. 'They would have been living in a log cabin until the stone cottage was built in 1879 or 1880,' says Betty Lewis today. Like many of the early settlers, the Ashhursts gardened for survival, planting fruit trees in the alluvial fields surrounding the creek. Gnarled specimens of medlar and persimmon remain from these earliest days. The original cottage, where the Ashhurst sons climbed a ladder to their bedroom, was extended by the next owner, Margaret Murray, who bought the property in 1936.

The bones of the 1.5-hectare garden that exists today were laid out by Miss Murray, who would draw lines on the ground with her walking stick to show where the paths and walls were to be built. Three massive terraces were created down the side of the mountain to the east of the house by an Italian and an Australian stonemason. Two sorts of stone were used; there is smooth stone from Tungkillo in the Adelaide Hills, some 50 kilometres from the property, as well as a rough stone from Wistow, the same distance in the opposite direction. The house is built in another local stone, its mellow tones offset perfectly along one side by the golden-apricot blooms of the repeat-flowering climbing rose 'Crepuscule'.

The collections of trees at Mount George, many of which were planted by Miss Murray, provide spectacular autumn displays. There are the yellows of the catalpa, close to the house, and the oranges and reds of the tupelos (*Nyssa sylvatica*) and the witchhazels (*Hamamelis mollis*), as well as the rare American leatherwood, *Cyrilla racemiflora*.

Of particular interest are several claret ash surviving from the first claret ash ever discovered. In 1910, a Mr T. C. Wollaston, who lived close by at Raywood, bought from his local nursery a wine-coloured ash seedling. He raised it at his property, cuttings were taken, and the claret ash was born. In 1926, a specimen was sent to Kew gardens where it was named *Fraxinus oxycarpa* 'Raywood'. Seen behind a stand of golden ash, the claret ash at Mount George are spectacular in April and May.

The top terrace is planted with roses; lots of old fashioned roses planted by Margaret Murray remain, along with the Lewis' choice of the more modern 'Apricot Nectar', 'Fragrant Cloud' and 'Iced Ginger'. Sections of the terraces are newly edged with the lavender, *Lavandula angustifolia* 'Nana' which has thrived over other cultivars in the Hills' climate.

Many will empathise with Betty Lewis when she attests 'I am not a plant expert but the plants give me great joy, and I do love the pictures they create in the garden.'

Opposite: Arrival at Mount George.

Below: The autumn colours of a catalpa backed with *Nyssa sylvatica* and *Parrotia persica*.

Bottom left: The repeat-flowering rose 'Crepuscule' is trellised on to the house.

How this garden works

* The five species of witchhazel (*Hamamelis* spp.) add colour in autumn as well as scented flowers in winter. In Trevor Nottle's Hills' garden, *Hamamelis* x *intermedia* 'Jelena' is prized for its leaves which turn oranges and reds and its bronzed, fragrant winter flowers.

* *Cyrilla racemiflora* is also grown for its scented white flowers, which emerge just before the new leaves of early spring.

Paradise transformed

The far north coast of New South Wales possesses a collection of unique charms: one of Australia's most beautiful beaches, charming villages set in picture-postcard dairy rich country, and a hinterland offering spectacular views up and down an azure coast.

Landscape designer Tim Hays says gardening in paradise presents particular challenges, however. For a start, says Tim, there is so much choice in plant material and styles. 'You can go temperate or tropical, but you have to be careful not to end up with a mish-mash. People who come here from Queensland want a garden of temperate plants, and people from Sydney or Melbourne want a tropical garden. I like to give people what they want, but I advise on what will grow well here.'

The gardens that Tim designs rely on deep beds, densely planted with suitable material, viewed from winding paths, usually of gravel. 'I try to eliminate as much lawn as possible, as in summertime here in the sub-tropics, you are mowing every week. I can think of much better things to do with your time and mine. If you plant out a garden properly, with the right balance of plants, you really don't need to do too much gardening. It's just a matter of cutting things back here and there.'

Up on Friday Hut Road, with its heady mix of mysterious scents and its dark and dappled light, is the garden of transplanted Sydneysiders, Jennifer Reagan and John Bennett. Again, Tim has designed an easy-care garden that relies on deep beds resplendant with thriving tropical plants that replace the traditional lawn.

As you enter the garden, the scene is set by a mass of flowering gingers, heliconias and the dramatic 'bird of paradise', *Strelitzia reginae*. You push past beds of flowering pentas, dietes, and the dwarf date

Tim's gardens require no irrigation, and rely entirely on natural rainfall. The gravel paths double as large drains. 'They catch all the rainwater, which then circulates into the garden beds of rich basalt soil; the plants feed from the roots up. I sometimes run the gravel a bit further off the paths, and under the garden beds, so that the water reaches all the plants immediately.'

Standing at the front of the house, you might observe that the lines of this garden are semi-circular. You look, from the house, against the setting sun, across the canopy of the rainforest, to the rolling hills. The bending branches of frangipani frame each side of the picture; the curving patterns are repeated in the garden beds. You are most certainly in paradise.

Opposite: *Pentas lanceolata* backed with *Heliconia bihai*.

Left: You watch the setting sun against a backdrop of rainforest and rolling hills.

Below: *Rhoeo spathacea*.

palm, *Phoenix roebelenii*, backed with *Heliconia bihai* looking something like a giant banana tree, the dense, green foliage offset by brilliant orange and red flowers. There is the summer flowering golden penda (*Xanthostemon chrysanthus*), a rainforest tree from North Queensland, its yellow blooms contrasting with the red powder-puff blossoms of the Mexican *Calliandra*.

A canopy over the entire garden is created by the yellow-flowered *Schizolobium parahybum*. This tree, native to the Brazilian rainforest, where it flowers at the same time as the jacaranda, is one of the fastest growing trees in the world, becoming massive in 20 years. Despite being sold in this country as the Mexican tree-fern tree, this is definitely not for the small garden.

The wooden house is designed to fit with the landscape and to afford views into the different corners of the garden. From the bathroom the owners look out onto a jungle of bromeliads, the flamboyant *Heliconia rostrata*, as well as foliage plants such as the zebra plant, *Calathea zebrina*, with its striped, emerald-green leaves backed with purple, brilliantly-coloured cordylines and cycads. One of Tim's principles is to carefully place leaf shapes and textures together. 'Gardens are not in flower all the time,' he says. 'The colour green is also important.'

Corinda

Wilmar Bouman fell in love with Corinda, an 1880s house set in the Hobart suburb of Glebe, 15 years ago, when he arrived from Holland, after looking around the world for the perfect place to settle. In 1992, Wilmar, an acclaimed floral artist, along with decorator and restorer Matthew Ryan, bought the house and set about a massive restoration project.

A large-scale renovation plan was also needed in the garden; privet hedges, cotoneaster and pittosporum had to be removed. A weeping willow, higher than the house, and with a trunk 1.5 metres in diameter, was taken down over two days, revealing a mature bull bay magnolia, which was to provide the inspiration for the colours of the house.

The garden is made up of several very different areas; there are formal areas, a woodland, shade gardens and a new winter border that uses plants in burgundies, pinks, greys and lime-green. Mathew Ryan has created a unique feel in each area by the use of differently textured materials for the garden paths; there is cobbling, mudstone, sandstone, bark, pebbles and convict brick. Great use is made of box hedges, some of which are very old; Wilmar has successfully broken a basic rule by cutting back ruthlessly into very old wood!

The front garden is dominated by an ambitious pleached lime walk in the shape of a large U. This is underplanted by a hedge of box and encloses a large circular bed divided into four. The two beds diagonally opposite each other house perennials in tones of pinks and blues. The other two beds house yellows; there are iris, yarrow and cream poppies.

'Because of my European background I like formality, but I don't want to be too serious. I like the garden to be full of surprises,' says Wilmar. A local artist has created wire frames for a menagerie of box topiary indigenous animals in different poses. There is a Tasmanian devil chasing four native hens that are running along in different stances. A European-style garden that is, therefore, uniquely Australian.

The front boundary of the garden is lined with the most successful hedge of 'Iceberg' that you are ever likely to see, reached through a beautifully designed iron arbor swamped with climbing 'Iceberg' roses and underplanted with alliums. Here, a 'gardener's cottage', built from timbers salvaged from an 1830s farm cottage that was about to be demolished, provides additional guest accommodation in such a beautiful setting that there is a danger that you won't really want to venture far.

In the shade of a screen of clipped yew along one side of the property are beds of hostas, underplanted with thousands of galanthus, and other shade-loving plants. Here the new border of colour and texture provides further intrigue throughout winter. There are the deep burgundies of *Euphorbia dulcis* 'Chameleon' and *Dianthus barbatus*

'Nigrescens', along with *Pittosporum* 'Tom Thumb', which is also terrific for hedging. There are the greys of sedums, senecias and ornamental artichokes and the lime-greens of some of the hostas.

'When developing the garden I looked at the shapes and colours of the plants. And we also work with a lot of coloured foliage. I'm not good with botanic names; I don't collect plants for their rarity, but for their looks.'

Wilmar Bouman, who trained in Holland for three years, and is a qualified teacher of floral decoration, has plenty of tips on arranging, and making flowers last. 'One of the main things with flowers is to plunge them into water; use chicken wire to support stems, rather than an oasis, where the uptake of water is insufficient.' A dash of bleach in the water will kill bacteria and keep vases clean. Wilmar puts sugar into the water when sprays are mostly still in bud. This provides the energy required for the buds to open.

Opposite left: Corinda was built in the 1880s in the Hobart suburb of Glebe.

Opposite right: The gardener's cottage, where you can stay.

Bottom left: Pots, clipped hedges and Iceberg roses.

Bottom right: *Hydrangea petiolaris*.

Kibbenjelok

The French explorer Antoine-Raymond-Joseph D'Entrecasteaux left France in 1791 to search for his missing compatriat Comte Jean-Francois de La Perouse, who had sailed into Botany Bay on 24 January 1788, four days after the arrival of the First Fleet. While the French Revolution was raging, D'Entrecasteaux was charting the Tasmanian waters. The beautiful D'Entrecasteaux Peninsula is an hour and a half south of Hobart; it was along this rugged coastline that the nineteenth century trading ships collected for ballast the tree ferns that now contribute so much to the exotic warm-climate gardens in the south of England.

It is here also that garden visitors will find Kibbenjelok, a 3-hectare garden around an 1890s farmhouse, created over the past 12 years by owners Gay and Kees Klok. Land that once housed apple orchards is today host to a marvellous collection of rare, cold-climate trees which create a cool canopy for the delicate treasures thriving beneath. 'I have a passion for species rhododendron,' says Gay Klok. 'I love the purity of the flower, the exciting leaf form—and most are scented. We also grow many different forms of Japanese maples, which excel in the moist, cool conditions. And forget-me-nots, species geraniums and foxgloves are allowed to romp away.'

Kibbenjelok houses a collection of magnolias—there is the extraordinary *Magnolia campbellii* 'Charles Raffill', which flowers much sooner than the 20 years it takes the species to blossom. The related *Michelia* extend the winter-to-spring flowering of the magnolias into early summer. There is also a rare weeping form of the Japanese 'Katsura tree', *Cercidiphyllum japonicum* 'Pendulum', and a collection of dogwoods, as well as of *Enkianthus*, small trees grown for their autumn colour.

Another woodland area shelters several varieties of silver birch. There is the very collectable *Betula albo-sinensis*, with its peeling, papery pink bark and form suited to growing in copses; it was discovered by the plant hunter Ernest 'Chinese' Wilson in China, in 1901. There is the birch with the whitest of bark of all—*Betula utilis* var. *jacquemontii*, perfect as a specimen tree or in an herbaceous border.

Shaded walks take the visitor past swathes of the coveted and temperamental blue Himalayan poppy, *Meconopsis betonicifolia*, and of candelabra primulas (*Primula pulverulenta*), in a dramatic and effective array of pinks and oranges, enjoying a moist, humus-rich position beneath massed tree ferns.

While Gay is not a rose fanatic, she does grow heritage and species roses for the excitement of their scarlet hips which contrast with the brilliant branches of nearby coral-bark maples (*Acer palmatum* 'Senkaki') and the 'wire-netting bush', *Corokia cotoneaster*, with its tracery of tangled branches and red berries giving pleasure in the midst of winter.

'I was like a child opening Christmas presents when we started this adventure,' says Gay. 'I could plant trees, with no limit on space—but I

learnt very early to stop planting one of each thing I liked. Now, I always plant in odd numbers—one, three or five—and hope that one won't die!'

She makes no plans on paper. 'I can always see the garden in my mind and I will sit the plant in various positions until I know it's right. Many I placed for autumn colouring—and the shape of a tree is of primary importance.'

Water in the garden is also crucial. 'We are still landscaping here, but I intend to keep the planting fairly simple, the view of the Channel and South Bruny Island taking the important role.' A large ornamental lake enhances this view and seems to bring it into the garden.

Opposite: A woodland walk at Kibbenjelok.

Above: An enviable collection of *Primula pulverulenta* multiplies at Kibbenjelok.

Left: Tree ferns are at home in this garden.

127

Gardens are for people

You'd expect Don Burke's garden to be good, wouldn't you? The man who brought 'infotainment' to Australian television, and gardening to everyone, has some very definite ideas, which he puts across each week, very succinctly. And he has a terrific garden.

How does an expert start a new project? 'You don't start in your garden,' he says. 'You drive around the neighbourhood and look at what grows well. Hydrangeas grew incredibly well here, so we knew we could put them in and that they would form the backbone of the garden.

'When buying a site, look at the cuttings in the road, at the soil profile. Check the rainfall.'

Don first designed his garden on paper. 'Always get a professional to help with the design,' he advises. 'Decide what you want from your garden. Do you want an area to sit; do you want a pool? Gardens are like kitchens—they have to work. Do a sketch, cut out the elements, roughly to scale, and try moving them around on your piece of paper. So you might say, "I can see the swimming pool from the kitchen window." And look at the "goat tracks". See where the kids go—that's where the paths should be. The plants are the easiest bit—you just tell your nurseryman the size and colour you need. The plants are just the parsley in the butcher shop window—just the garnish. It's the design that makes the garden work, not the plants.'

Don says the English-designed gardens are to be looked at, not lived in. 'We have copied English gardens that don't work for our climate and our needs. And I am president, and all the members of, the "I hate pergolas foundation". They are useless; a verandah and roof is much better. The Spanish have worked all this out.'

carpet effect.' A low informal hedge of the *Rhododendron* 'Christmas Cheer' planted behind, frames and accentuates the arc-shaped plantings.

The camellia 'Marj Miller' is planted elsewhere on banks and is, in Don's view, the most important camellia ever bred. 'It will cascade down a bank; it's most useful as a groundcover.'

A bank in front of the house is covered in hundreds of azaleas. At the top is 'Red Wing', followed by 'Rose Queen'; at the bottom of the slope is 'White Prince'. These are azaleas which, according to Don, 'don't die and are great for landscaping'.

Don planted 'sacks and sacks of daffodils and jonquils'—more than 5000—in whites and creams. 'One of everything almost never looks good. I know it's hard when you love plants to use lots of the one thing. I am a bowerbird too, but I try to discipline myself.'

And Don loves perfumed plants. 'That's where the magic comes from.'

Opposite: Don Burke has used 'lots of the one thing' in his mountain garden.

Left: Whimsy and magic are important in any garden.

Below: The glorious colours of maples.

Whimsy and magic are important to Don Burke. 'Gardens are for families, for children and for enjoyment, for the re-creation of your spirit. They are not about winning a garden competition. They should have magic and fun.'

The theme of Don's garden is Alice in Wonderland. 'I still appreciate childlike things. If an adult loses that, he has lost an important part of his soul,' he says. Throughout the garden 'Alice-sculptures' are hidden among the mass plantings of ajuga, aluminium plant and dwarf camellias. '"Baby Bear" is one of the great camellias of the twentieth century; it's very slow growing, but produces a mass of dainty pink flowers. It's very dense, and perfect for hedging.'

In Don's garden the slopes he inherited have been planted with different species of hydrangea. 'The hollows are filled with the old fashioned, big hydrangeas; on the crests are the smaller hydrangeas. They grow in full sun and they don't get pruned. In sun they grow very densely; it's only in shade that they grow spindly.' Planted behind, to tumble down the bank, is a sweep of the weeping form of *Nyssa sylvatica*.

Beneath is a clever garden of varieties of Japanese maple (*Acer dissectum*) looking like giant, rounded boulders. 'You don't see them as maples, you just read the shape,' Don says. Underneath, a lawn of 50 different varieties of white, pink, purple and blue violets is mown several times each year. 'With the different foliage colours, you get a Persian

Pruning

Pruning is a subject which occupies gardeners' thoughts at regular intervals throughout the year. Long before winter one might fret about how to prune the long walk of apples. Should it be pruned low, so that picking and maintaining are easier, or should the crown of each of the 60 trees be lifted, creating a cathedral of meeting branches, such as at Brooke Cottage in England's Cotswolds?

Studies of medieval monastery gardens can lead to the yearning for a pear tunnel: you need to have your iron support in place before you plant, and to start pruning and shaping from 'day one'. A garden room with walls of hazelnuts, trimmed annually into a 'loose hedge', and where you can go to hide or to read a book, will, after just a few years of growth, also yield kilos of delicious nuts each March.

The red-stemmed dogwood, *Cornus alba* 'Sibirica', one of the joys of the winter garden (if you can stop it running riot), should be cut down to the ground after you've enjoyed its glowing red stems in the winter border.

Perhaps the most satisfying task of all is cutting the faded leaves from the hellebores in summer, so that the winter flowers emerge fresh and pristine in July, when there is little else to enjoy or pick.

Even pruning the roses has its joys—again, there is that sense of a job well done. The once-only 'heritage' roses should be pruned after flowering and then left to grow long canes, which can be pegged down or tied together to provide a mad froth of flowers the following November.

Lavenders—so perfect with roses—must be clipped regularly right from planting if you want to avoid unsightly bare legs. Sacrifice flowers the first year and prune for a thick plant. Then prune after flowering, cleaning up the clippings to constantly 'grow on' replacement plants.

At Flutes Restaurant, set within the Brookland Valley Vineyard in the Margaret River, a 10-year-old 'Sauvignon Blanc' vine is espaliered over one wall of the winery boutique. As in the vineyard, each winter spur pruning is carried out to remove the previous year's fruiting canes. New growth is tied in place and all downward facing shoots are removed. All remaining canes are shortened to two or three buds.

When it comes to wisterias, Dr Peter Valder is a world authority; he recommends hard pruning straight after flowering. 'After that, tip prune long suckers and tie them in the required position. Once you have the growth and cover you want, prune all new shoots to two or three leaves, thus encouraging the development of the flower spurs.

'All suckers and unwanted shoots are most easily removed as they appear, as they come away easily when pulled ... while still young and soft,' Peter advises, assuring us that 'on reaching maturity the production of new shoots lessens annually and the task becomes much less time-consuming'.

Left: Lavender thrives at the entrance to the Brookland Valley Vineyard.

Cycad country

Stories that Peter Heirbloem tells of photographing and studying cycads, in some of the world's more remote and dangerous countries, bring to mind the feats of the intrepid plant hunters and botanists of the nineteenth century who braved unthinkable conditions to give us the thousands of plants we now take for granted.

During his travels through Africa, Peter, something of a new millennium Indiana Jones, made friends with the Swahili-speaking pygmies of Zaire, now properly called the Democratic Republic of Congo. Ignoring their poisoned arrows, he cut through unexplored jungle, and dealt with truculent officials at border crossings.

'The friend with whom I travelled belongs to the Landrover club of Nairobi, and they're a pretty adventurous group,' admits Peter. 'But when he told his friends that he was going into Zaire they thought he was joking, and then they thought he was crazy.' Explaining the passion that prompts him to regularly risk his life, he says, 'They're living fossils, they haven't changed in 180 million years'.

The cycads for which Peter searches are rare and endangered. 'One colony, in Zaire, has only been visited two or three times in history,' he says. 'The pygmies took us along their walking track where the jungle was so dense that at midday it was almost pitch black.'

In Mozambique, he went in search of the obscure *Encephalartos turneri*. 'That country is almost unvisited,' he says. 'There are landmines everywhere; all the bridges are out. Forget telephones.'

In South Africa all cycads in the wild are microchipped. 'You're arrested if you are found with any illegal plants. There, you need a permit just to move a cycad, even in your own garden,' he warns.

Peter has exchanged cycads with many botanic gardens around the world including South Africa's Lowveld Botanic Garden and Ewanrigg Botanic Garden in Harare, where the most extensive collection of African cycads in the world is kept. 'We've done three exchanges over a period of five years,' he says. 'And I've sent them 80 species of Australian, Mexican and Central American cycads.'

At his cycad garden and nursery, Eudlo Cycad Gardens, in the hinterland of Queensland's Sunshine Coast, 3 hectares of landscaped rockeries are home to over 2000 cycads comprising more than 230 species as well as more than 150 species of palms and a massive collection of succulents and euphorbias. His particular interest is in the cycads of Central and Southern Africa and his collection includes endangered species such as *Encephalartos lebombonsis*, from South Africa.

Peter insists there is a place for cycads in the home garden. 'People just don't know about them,' he says. 'Cycads mix well with other plants, but are also good on their own, massed.'

Below: *Encephalartos lebombonsis*.

Wildflowers

We are driving north from Perth on the Brand Highway to Western Australia's Mid West region. It is mid August and we're heading toward the small township of Eneabba in search of the famed wildflowers. I am extremely fortunate in having Claire Welsh, a past president of the Wildflower Society of Western Australia, as my guide.

As we drive the seemingly endless highway, Claire tells me about the plants we are passing. Just out of Perth, the flora consists of banksia woodland. There is also the prickly barked coastal blackbutt (*Eucalyptus todtiana*) as well as Christmas trees (*Nuytsia floribunda*), and grevilleas growing alongside the hibbertias. 'Not anything terribly showy,' says Claire Welsh—but it's all there, just as it has been for millions of years.

There are also pale swathes of smoke bush, *Conospermum* spp., thought to have possible curative properties for cancer. (The locals are keeping quiet about the species so people don't descend to rip it out of the bush.)

There is also *Dryandra sessilis*, a favourite with the beekeepers, because it flowers in the winter and produces a unique honey. It is growing with *Stipa elegantissima*. As the species name suggests, this is a very elegant little grass which sports white plumes; it's popular for Perth gardens.

Eucalyptus macrocarpa, with its large silver leaves and spectacular red flowers and fruit, is indigenous to these northern sand plains. It is

very sought after for flower arrangements and for export to Japan, along with Blue boy (*Stirlingia latifolia*), named after Sir James Stirling, first Governor of Western Australia, from 1829 to 1832 and again from August 1834 until December 1838. (The roots of the Blue boy give off a blue dye which stains the sands in which the plant grows. 'If you were a plasterer and you sourced your sands from an area which grows Blue boy, your customers would end up with blue streaks in their walls, which are impossible to remove,' explains Claire.)

About three hours north of Perth we turn right off the Brand Highway and climb, along a red dirt road, to the Yandin Hill Lookout. The 15-minute walk around the Yandin reserve is most welcome; look carefully and you will find tiny donkey orchids, many species of hibbertia and the low-growing cat's paw (*Anigozanthos humilis*). All around are the native grass trees, *Xanthorroea preissii*. We look down and out onto the northern wheatbelt and towards the beautiful Batavia Coast and the astonishing turquoise colours of the Indian Ocean. From the lookout we can also see the ancient volcanic formation of flat topped hills which go by the geological name of Mesa. One of them, Mount Lesure, rich in flora, is a 'must' for another adventure.

We continue on, along the Brand Highway, past a mass of the brilliant blue *Lechenaultia biloba*, growing with the buttercup-yellow *Hibbertia hypericoides*. A little further north are wide expanses of *Banksia hookerana*, also a favourite for cut flowers.

Further north and further east is station country and the mulga woodland area. The red sandy loam is covered with carpets of wildflowers which have been stimulated by the first autumn rains. The show will go on into September and even October, if it's a lucky season and there are good follow-up rains.

The everlasting daisies, in particular, form a finely detailed tapestry of pinks, whites, yellows and blues, so spectacular that we make slow progress as we constantly leap from the car to photograph—but that's a story for another time.

Opposite: *Lechenaultia biloba* grows alongside *Hibbertia hypercoides*.

Above: The exquisite blossom of *Eucalyptus macrocarpa*.

Left: Everlasting daisies create a carpet of colour near Eneabba.

Sacred ground

One of several great joys of writing about, and photographing, gardens in Australia, is coming to understand the power of this country. You can be moved to tears by the strength of the Australian landscape as you cut across a mountain range and look down from on high—eagles soaring overhead—onto a patchwork of brown, tilled soil alongside paddocks of golden sunflowers or canola. You can't help but be impressed by the spirit of Australians when you visit gardens which have been restored after bushfire, have coped with drought and then with floods as well as with the constant uncertainty of distant markets.

The Taroom Shire is a five-hour drive north-west of Goondiwindi and the Queensland–New South Wales border. The properties here are of rich black soil, river flats or productive brigalow country, tightly held by a few families. One such property is The Glebe, now of 4000 hectares, bound along its northern side by the Dawson River.

When I visited in September 1997, the district was enduring its tenth year of drought; 175 millimetres of rain had fallen the entire year and cattle picked among sparse twigs of grass in the vast landscape.

Christine Gall's grandfather, George Beaumont Rigby, arrived in the area from England, in 1876. In 1900 he bought three leases totalling 26 000 acres (10 000 hectares) from the larger Cockatoo Station. With his wife and six children, he lived in a tent on the home block that he named The Glebe, while he built a rough dwelling, which was to be followed by the present house in 1915.

The house, built out of Moreton Bay ash (*Eucalyptus tessellaris*) is constructed in the simple style of a mid-nineteenth century dwelling, of horizontal slabs of sawn, un-dressed timber. Built in two sections joined by a breezeway, the house is classified by The National Trust.

Country women today have to turn their hand to a vast number of tasks. 'These days we do just about anything and everything,' says Christine Gall cheerily. 'Most of the women do that. It wasn't the case years ago, of course. Today we do the books, and help with the mustering and the ploughing.' And yet they all make time for gardening.

Perhaps the most striking feature of the garden at The Glebe is the three massive jacaranda planted at the turn of the century by George Rigby's eldest daughter. They thrive, even in the tough years, to flower a deep lavender-blue, each October. Several old bougainvillea give a brilliant display each September, with a purple variety seemingly unique to old Queensland country homesteads. 'The bougainvillea is pruned back when we get the time,' says Christine Gall. 'Often with the cattle dehorners as the canes are so thick and tough.'

This unique house and garden are filled with the spirits of pioneering women—but Christine is worried that this heritage may be lost. If the proposed Nathan Dam, which would cover some 15 000 hectares of prime grazing land and submerge 14 properties, goes ahead, the important house would have to be moved—and much of Queensland's early history would be gone forever.

Left: The bougainvilleas at The Glen give a brilliant display.

Bromeliad bounty

Bromeliads seem to be a well-kept secret. Perhaps they are just too exotic, perhaps too architectural, perhaps they suffer, like so many plants, from being inadvisably used.

They are, however, extremely useful plants in difficult situations—in a narrow, dark, hard-to-reach area between two houses, in deep shade, and in situations where the other plants are greedy. They need little water—none at all in winter—and they grow in little or no soil. They display marvellous contrasts in colour, texture and shape in the foliage and, just as a bonus, the flowers last for months.

Lindsay Gerchow and Danny Yves are extremely passionate about bromeliads. 'We came across this marvellous collection a few years ago, and we said "that's it; that's our vocation",' says Lindsay. 'They've taken us all over the world since.'

The two garden at Buderim, on the Sunshine Coast hinterland; in 1999 their garden, Bellrive, was awarded grand champion for the area. Since buying their property, they have extended into the neighbouring garden to provide additional breeding and space for their collection.

'Bromeliads have only been known, really, in the last 20 years,' says Danny. 'During the war many collectors sent their treasures out to Australia. There are now an enormous number of Australian hybrids, crossed with bromeliads from all over the world.'

Bromeliads are no demanding, fractious prima donnas. 'But don't have them in the midday sun,' says Lindsay. 'The coarser leaved bromeliads, like the *Neoregelia* genus, can take more sun, the softer leaved less sun, and they don't like frost. The more intense the colour, the more sun they can take.' *Neoregelia* 'Prince of Darkness' and *N. Meyendorfii* x *inferno* are favourites. *N.* 'Perfection' is nearly black and sports brown and red stripes. The boys are on the look out for *Neoregeilia* 'Star of Bethlehem', a hybrid with plain green leaves and red tips that seems to have disappeared from cultivation.

Lindsay and Danny pay tribute to Grace Goode, a breeder now 83 years of age, who introduced them to the plant group. 'She started off with just one, then she started to experiment, and then got hooked,' says Danny. Among the hybrids Grace has developed are *Neoregilia* 'Charm', *N.* 'Gold Fever' and *N.* 'Amazing Grace', lime-green with cerise stripes.

Bromeliads can be grown in potting mix or orchid mix, don't need fertilising, and rarely need watering. 'The cups catch the rainwater. In the Amazon, the cups are so large the frogs lay their eggs in the water collected there,' adds Lindsay.

Above: Grace Goode hybrid 'Sheer Joy'.

Treasure hunting

Gardeners often wonder what it is that makes them obsessive. Is it the thrill of the chase for the rare or new plant? Is it the desire for what one can't have—plants suited to a different climate? Is it the wonderful, sudden realisation that there is something of the artist in each of us? Most of us can't collect or create great art or architecture—but beauty is within reach. Each of us can create a garden.

Otto Fauser is a plant hunter, searching the world for rare treasures. His treks through catalogues received from societies around the world are as rewarding as those of the hunters of old who risked their lives to bring new plants to the west.

Otto's garden, Doshong La, is named after the mountain pass in south-eastern Tibet where plant hunter Frank Kingdom-Ward found 20 alpine *Rhododendron* species, out of more than 100 he discovered in his 47-year career. He called the pass 'Rhododendron Fairyland'.

Otto Fauser hunts from his mountain garden, and his collections are arranged in a series of terraces, retained by granite boulders. Large rocks also provide a growing base for plants such as the Hungarian *Daphne blagayana*, clinging to the rock. Nearby is the alpine groundcover *Daphne arbuscula*, from the Czech Republic, placed at waist height and near steps so the scent can be appreciated.

Otto's passion includes alpine plants, crocus, fritillarias and other small bulbs, many grown in raised beds, so that the extraordinary markings on their diminutive faces can be seen, and to ensure the perfect drainage they demand. Otto raises bulbs from seed received from botanical and private gardens throughout the world.

The hardy slipper orchids from Japan (*Cypripedium japonicum* var.

formosanum) imported as rhizomes, now look extraordinary, massed at the base of a tree stump at Doshong La. Nearby, clumps of the Japanese woodland iris (*Iris gracilipis*), a powder-blue, thrive, as does the more unusual white form.

The garden houses over 150 species of rhododendron. Clinging to some of the rocks are rare treasures such as the tiny *R. forrestii*, which is found at over 4500 metres in Tibet and Burma.

Toward the bottom of the garden, *Trillium rivale* flourishes in the humus rich soil with erythroniums and fritillarias. The last fritillaria to flower is the black sarana—(*Fritillaria camschatcensis*) from the moist sub-alpine meadows of Alaska and Asia. From Greece comes the extraordinary black *Fritillaria tuntasia*.

Creating collections, and becoming an expert at growing certain plants, is part of the 'pull' of gardening. While we can't all own a collection of important paintings, searching for old and rare botanical books is exciting, and accessible. Otto Fauser's collection includes issues of the hand-coloured *Curtis' Botanical Magazine*, from 1779.

So where do you start? Firstly, get to know a good bookseller. Dr Elizabeth Kerr (no relation), of Garden Street Books, advises collecting around your area of interest. 'Have a wants list,' she says. 'The plant hunters make fascinating collecting. Roses are a huge area. However, it's not necessary to buy every book in your chosen subject.'

Liz believes you must be fussy about the condition of a book. 'After a while you can recognise whether a book is in its original condition,' she says. 'By the same token, if you can only get something imperfect, but it is important for your collection, buy it—and replace it later. Also, buy a later edition of an important book, if that's what you can afford, and upgrade to a first edition. You can start off very simply, and replace each piece of your collection as it becomes possible.'

Opposite left: Hardy slipper orchids from Japan (*Cypripedium japonicum* var. *formosanum*) imported as rhizomes, look extraordinary, massed at the base of a tree stump at Doshong La.
Opposite right: The garden houses more than 150 species of rhododendron.
Above: Otto Fauser's passion includes alpine plants, crocus, fritillarias and other small bulbs.

A winter garden

In the centre of Adelaide, in Millswood, is a tiny garden packed with the botanical treasures of plant collectors Don Barrett and Harvey Collins. Every centimetre of this inner-city space is used to house an intellectual —and eclectic—array of plants from every corner of the globe. The boundary walls and fences of the garden are covered in lattice for vertical planting and Victorian wire plant stands make free use of the air!

The garden mainly features winter flowering plants. 'We're lazy in summer,' says Don. First to flower as the weather turns chilly is the genus *Oxalis*; the collection here includes over 70 species. When I visited in late autumn *Oxalis gracilis* was a mass of fabulous apricot-coloured flowers.

In August the hellebores are putting on their annual show. There is *Helleborus vesicarius*, from Turkey, which earns a place because of its fabulous seed pods. There is the long-flowering *H.* x *nigercors*, a cross between the species niger and argutifolius, and which can produce up to 34 blooms on one stem. *H.* x *ballardiae* is a cross between niger and lividus and is most collectable because of its cream flowers which turn dark pink. The coveted gold-leaved form of *H. foetidus* was grown from seed sent by a British collector.

There is lots to wish for in the clivia collection, apart from the popular cream-flowering species. There is the rare *C. gardenii*, with its pendulous flowers that have green tips and which tone to yellow and orange.

You can't help wondering just what it is that motivates the collector. 'Some people collect plants like others collect stamps,' says Don. 'It's the chase. We all want what we can't have!'

Because the garden houses each of the 19 species of cyclamen, except for *C. somalense*, which was only recently discovered in Somalia, there is a cyclamen in flower each month of the year. The calendar starts in March with *hederifolium*, including *C. h.* 'Bowle's Apollo', then carpets of *C. coum* bloom through winter. *Cyclamen rohlsfianum*, from Libya, is, according to Barrett, 'almost impossible to flower. We've had one bloom'.

In spring *Cyclamen repandum* performs, with its curled petals and exquisite marbled leaves, followed by the evergreen *C. purpurascens* along with *C. trochopteranthum*. There is also *C. cyprium* 'Elizabeth Strangman'; her dark leaves display exquisite white spotting.

'As this is a tiny garden, we also have a collection of miniature narcissus, including the autumn flowering *Narcissus viridiflora*, which flowers in autumn and smells of 1808 hair oil,' says Harvey Collins. Also flowering in autumn is the tiny *N. serotinus*, from Spain.

A north wall shelters the stunning baby pink flowers of *Brugmansia* 'Equador Pink'; *B.* 'Grand Marnier' has salmon pink flowers with a wide 'skirt'. The garden also houses rare double yellow and double purple flowered daturas (known as *Datura* until recently) all of which have been grown from seed.

At the end of spring the tree peonies are gearing up for their annual exhibition, with *Paeonia suffruticosa* 'Destiny' a favourite. This easy-to-grow single peony has large white flowers with a burgundy centre.

So what now, I ask? 'There is always the next thing to move on to,' says Don, who has just received a new plant catalogue from the United Kingdom. 'We won't be able to resist some new treasure,' he admits, with a wistful sigh.

Opposite: *Cyclamen persicum*.

Above: Millswood's tiny garden is packed with botanical treasures.

Left: The succulents collection in the courtyard.

How this garden works

* In the Millswood garden, nerines, including the apricot-coloured 'Aurora', grow where there is no irrigation system—needing to be bone dry throughout summer.

* To encourage germination, cyclamen seed must be steeped in quite hot water which is mixed with a little detergent for two or three days.

Mornington magic

A sweeping drive of the lemon-scented gum that thrives in the Mornington Peninsula area leads into Jenny and Cyril Lansell's 2.5-hectare garden which is set within their cattle property, Willawong, 60 minutes south of Melbourne.

A section of the long drive is also bordered by claret ash; several more are to be planted in the paddocks nearer to the house, thus bringing the landscape into the garden.

One of the first tasks that faced the Lansells when they bought Willawong two years ago was the reversal of the erosion that was degrading the creeks that run through the property. With the help and advice of Landcare Australia, three months were spent clearing out the creeks that were thick with blackberry and gorse: in August they will be fenced off to prevent cattle further damaging the fragile banks, and crossings for the cattle will be built up. 'This will encourage vegetation, which helps with our salinity problem, and will create a wildlife corridor,' says Jenny. 'We now have frogs, wood-duck and wild duck, and we hope the platypus will return.'

Massive earth moving has taken place over the past year; another dam has been dug because the water in the spring-fed lake, as well as in the creeks, is saline. The lake has been extended and deepened to over three metres in parts, to prevent foxes from reaching the centre island which is home to white Chinese geese and other birdlife. Three hundred she-oaks (*Allocasuarina*) have been planted leading down to the lake and the large species roses have been moved from the garden to this area, which can be seen from the verandahs of the house. A clear-red dash of the single-flowered rose 'Altissimo' sets off the

mauves, deep blues and the reds, rather than too much white,' she says. 'The rugosas are very successful down here. They are easy going and tough. They provide shelter for the other roses, and they don't need much water.'

Some courageous decisions have been taken: two 20-year-old camellias were moved. 'We did it with a tractor and ropes and six people, and extracted each with a massive root ball. We mulched madly, watered them in by keeping the hose trickling for days—and they've never looked back.'

Opposite: The deep-red English-bred 'L.D. Braithwaite' adds dash to a country garden.

Left: The rich red fruit of *Rosa scabrosa*.

Below: The crops in the vegetable garden are rotated regularly.

gumleaf colour of the house, which has a Mediterranean feel—perfect for its site.

Early attention was paid to drainage; over 8 kilometres of 'ag. Pipe' have been laid throughout the garden. 'The soil is rich but, being clay, the structure wasn't there, and the moisture had nowhere to go,' says Jenny.

On a level area behind the house is a covetable kitchen garden. Protected by olive hedges to the south and lattice—which also hides such essentials as the clothes line—to the west, this area is divided into six beds which provide vegetables and herbs year-round.

Broad beans, leeks, several different types of onions, as well as potatoes, carrots, spinach and winter lettuce, have just been planted. In August, Jenny will plant a bed of white stock, for picking. The beans, which are supported by tripods in summer, give way to sweet peas for winter scent and colour. Above the vegetable garden, and behind the olive hedges, the 'top lawn' has been rotary hoed and is now set with fruit trees which shade thousands of daffodils.

Windbreaks of hazelnuts and x *Cupressocyparis leylandii* and hedges of escallonia have been planted to create protection for the garden and a microclimate for some of the garden beds.

With trial and error Jenny has learned which roses will tolerate the saline conditions; her favourite rose is the very fragrant 'Limelight', as well as the rich red 'L.D. Braithwaite' and 'Othello', both bred by David Austin. 'I think a country garden needs the stronger colours, like the

How this garden works

* The lemon-scented gum *Eucalyptus citriodora* has been re-named *Corymbia citriodora*.

* Jenny Lansell plants her sweet peas in May.

* Hedges of the beautiful rugosa rose 'Alba' provide further protection for garden beds at Willawong.

* Aged horse manure comes from local racing stables, and is used as mulch around the fruit trees and on the vegetable beds.

Fairhill

Barbara Hansen believes that if plants can be coaxed to thrive on her site—on clay soil in the hinterland of Queensland's Sunshine Coast—they will grow almost anywhere in Australia. A hobby that started 25 years ago quickly became a passion and is now a thriving business. Fairhill displays Queensland's most comprehensive range of native plants; there are rainforest plantings, a river walk along the North Maroochy River, a wildflower meadow and a 'useful wild plant walk'.

The garden has been created on a remnant sugar cane plantation. 'Pretty horrible gear,' says the garden's rainforest expert, Phil Jobson. 'Sugar cane is a very aggressive crop. Takes everything out of the soil. We need to fertilise a lot. There's nothing wrong with clay soil, nutrition wise, but it has no structure. You put a plant in the soil and it just sits there, and when it rains it gets waterlogged. Mulch has made this garden.'

The first area created at Fairhill was the rainforest, and attention was paid immediately to establishing an essential canopy. Now, gorgeous gingers thrive, along with cordylines, and the elephant's ear, *Alocasia brisbanensis*. There are groundcovers like *Pollia crispata* and *Viola hederacea*, although this little native violet can go mad. There is *Freycinetia scandens* and *F. excelsor*, which scramble along the ground and climb trees; the white flower is followed by beautiful, strawberry-like fruit. There is *Zieria* 'Carpet Star', a tough and good looking form of this groundcover which is found in the sand dunes of northern New South Wales.

The plantings of eucalypts at Fairhill feature stunning new crosses bred by local plantsman Stan Henry, who was looking for a small flowering gum for the average-sized garden that could be grown through much of Australia. Henry has been crossing and grafting eucalypts for 20 years, when other experts maintained it couldn't be done. The cross between *Eucalyptus ptychocarpa* and *E. ficifolia* has resulted in *E.* 'Summer Red', which boasts a large head of red flowers, and *E.* 'Summer Beauty'.

Fairhill also holds a large collection of the bird-attracting grevillea. *Grevillea* 'Golden Lyre', a cross between 'Honey Gem' and *G. formosa*, grows to a height of 2 metres and has a spread of 5 metres. 'Golden Lyre' has long golden flowers for at least six months of the year, through summer and autumn and into winter in frost free environments. *Grevillea* 'Poorinda Royal Mantle' is a groundcover that is particularly successful on sunny, well drained banks or slopes, although it also tolerates heavy frosts.

In the wildflower garden there are paper daisies, flannel flowers and kangaroo paws, as well many plants being trialled for suitability to the climate. 'During spring the kangaroo paws put on a wonderful show. The flannel flowers, which seed easily, have become naturalised. They fit in beautifully with whatever other plants you are growing.'

Left: The rare black Kangaroo Paw (*Macropidia fuliginosa*).

Carpets of wildflowers

There are two things you must remember if you are planning a wildflower hunting adventure in Western Australia: you need local knowledge, and you must book ahead if you prefer to sleep between sheets.

If you drive about four hours north from Perth, and on through Eneabba, you will come to Allan and Lorraine Tinker's Western Flora Caravan Park. Originally from Victoria, self-taught plantsman Allan Tinker has run Western Flora for 10 years, welcoming thousands of enthusiasts who come from around the world in search of botanical treasure. Allan can point you in the direction of the best wildflower display, whichever week you arrive. 'This area should be known as the wildflower capital of the world,' he insists. 'Mount Lesueure, to the west of here—and named after the French botanist—has a greater number of flowering plants per square metre than anywhere in the world. It rivals the world-acclaimed Fynbos in South Africa.'

Tinker's 70-hectare Western Flora site, set on the north Eneabba sand plains, abounds with wildflowers. In August, you will find half-a-dozen species of native orchid, including the donkey orchid *Diuris porrifolia* and the rare Arrowsmith spider orchid *Caladenia crebra*. There is *Geleznowia verrucosa*; its flowers turn red after pollination to repel the now-obsolete bees.

Not far north is Coal Seam Gully, where coal was first mined in Western Australia. In late August, 40 different species of plants give a breathtaking effect. While the everlasting daisies flower from early July to the end of August, the peak time for a combination of wildflowers is usually the last week September to the first week in October, with the verticordias the last to bloom, in late November.

After the excitement of 'the Coal Seam' we were eager to discover more, and with Allan's advice, headed north-east, in search of the famous tapestries of groundcovering pastel colour. Confident with our recent success, we sauntered into the pub at Mullewa to request a room for the night. The bar fell silent; all eyes were upon us. The hotel was booked out and, after much ringing around, it seemed that the local gaol was the only alternative to our small, packed car. Tears of homesickness stung the eyes. Finally, the publican held his hand over the mouthpiece of the telephone—there was a bed in the shearers' quarters, up in 'station country', some 200 kilometres north-east. We didn't think twice.

The frantic drive, toward the setting sun, through the ghost town of Pindar and on, was not in vain—the bed aside. The never-ending straight road of deep red sand was bordered by endless expanses of wildflowers, swathes of pinks, whites, creams and yellows, as if a watercolourist had taken a broad sable brush with generous strokes across an ochre wash. There was *Velleia rosea*, with her white and mauve sisters, one of 14 species of velleia, forming the understorey to the pink everlastings, the white pompom everlastings and the yellow goodenias.

The next day, back past Pindar, heading south toward the town of Tardun and in mulga country, we were in search of the gravel pits which are now home to the wreath flower, *Lechenaultia macrantha*. This plant, indigenous to this mid west region, starts as little green bundles; then the prostrate stamens creep out along the sand, eventually sending up yellow and red terminal flowers. The older the plant gets, the bigger the wreath becomes, decorating the roadsides, and bringing traffic to a halt.

Below: Everlastings flower in the north-west from July to early September, in areas such as the Coal Seam Gully.

Spring

Sherwood

Excitement is mounting. The garden, which was pruned and clipped for winter, tidied and sprayed, mulched and put to bed, is ready to wake. The deciduous trees are unfurling lime-green, fresh new leaves; the first of the crabapples to flower, *Malus floribunda*, is ready to burst into coconut ice colours; and the wisteria is promising to cover the garden in scent. Spring is here. And it's almost rose time again.

At the foothills of The Grampians, in the Western District of Victoria, lies Sherwood, a stunning rose garden set within a working Murray Grey Stud and deer farm, owned by Geoff and Roma Campbell. Geoff's family has worked the property since 1926; the garden has been created since Geoff and Roma took over 44 years ago.

While there are many wonderful trees throughout the garden, roses are most definitely the Campbells' first love. The garden, which is just over 1 hectare, is home to more than 500 roses, which are at their peak in mid November.

Just inside the garden gate, that grand old tree of the Australian countryside, the river red gum (*Eucalyptus camaldulensis*) stands a kindly guard and attracts wonderful birdlife. The popular modern rose 'Sparrieshoop', bred in Germany in 1953 by Kordes and named after his local village, flowers repeatedly along one side of the drive. The generous trusses of blossom are pale pink and very perfumed. On the other side of the drive, a long bed of white hybrid musk roses greets the visitor. There is the beautiful, cream-coloured, fragrant 'Prosperity', bred by the Reverend Joseph Pemberton in 1919; there is the white-flowered and perfumed 'Pax', from the same breeder, released the year before; as well as the glorious 'Buff Beauty', which is covered in caramel to apricot flowers in summer and autumn.

A full range of the infamous David Austin (roses bred in England for old fashioned form and scent, but recurrent and displaying the hardiness of the moderns), includes the apricot 'Emmanuel', 'Graham Thomas', which is a glorious gold, the yellow-flowered 'Charles Austin' and pink 'Leander'. 'I love them all,' says Roma Campbell, 'although I'm not so keen on the reds.'

One of the most popular David Austin, the very full, apricot-coloured 'Abraham Darby', is among the beds burgeoning with gorgeous roses in perfect health. 'All the rose gardens in this district are wonderful,' says Roma. 'They love the openness of the area, and the months of dry summer heat.'

Roma's favourite roses are the modern 'Gold Medal' and the exquisitely shaped, peach-coloured 'Pink Parfait'. 'They are marvellous roses for picking. I love the colours and they look beautiful in the vase,' she says.

The garden also holds a collection of the roses bred by the Australian rosarian, Alister Clark, who set out to breed roses suited to the Australian climate, with its hot, dry summers. Sherwood houses one of Clark's greatest successes, the pink, semi-double climber 'Kitty Kininmonth' as well as 'Cicely Lascelles', a climber with semi-double, fragrant, apple pink blooms. 'These are really good, hardy, showy roses,' says Roma.

While the Western District boasts some of the country's greatest gardens, it can be difficult gardening country. At Sherwood, the sandy loam

has been enriched with manures and topsoil from the paddocks. 'The garden is very flat,' says Roma, 'so we've built up the beds for drainage, edging them in stones and logs from the property. Groundcovers and perennials such as catmint are encouraged to spill over.'

Walkways and arbours, built by Geoff and covered in climbing roses, direct the visitor on a gentle wander through this beautiful garden. In the background, and across simple, unobtrusive fences, are the ever-present, razor sharp and intensely blue Grampians. No garden could have a more breathtaking setting.

Opposite: The Grampians form a backdrop to the 'Gold Bunny' roses at Sherwood.

Above: The spreading form of river red gum in the Sherwood garden.

Left: The garden has a collection of roses bred by the Australian rosarian, Alister Clark, who set out to breed roses suited to the Australian climate.

How this garden works

* While many roses, including the David Austins, hybrid teas and floribundas, will have been pruned in winter, the old fashioned roses which flower only once, in late spring, are pruned after flowering has finished.

* Roma Campbell underplants her roses with bulbs and iris.

Tropical paradise

Close to the main street of Noosa, on Queensland's Sunshine Coast, is a garden of tropical splendour created over 15 years by lifelong gardener, Mary Collyer. Even at the end of winter her garden looks superb. Entering the garden is to dive into a world of fabulous colour and shape, arranged so successfully that it appears as if it has all just happened.

'I've been through the annual thing, the shrub thing and the pouring on the water thing,' says Mary. 'People say you can't grow anything in sandy soil,' she adds. 'We've got 12 metres of pure, white sand here, but I always think plants need good drainage, and if you mulch and fertilise … I don't think a cottage garden, nor roses, are for me here, so I decided I would have a foliage garden.'

The aspect of the garden is crucial. 'I chose this block because it's protected from the cold south-east by the hill, and we set the house back. The garden then faces due north, so it's warm and the tropical plants thrive. In winter we get sun till the last moment. I've been gardening for half a century; over the years you learn a lot.'

A massive Cooloola pine is the centrepiece of the front garden, providing shade for the tender plants and a home for soft-stem dendrobium orchids and trunk-hugging bromeliads. 'That pine attracted me to the block. It only grows from Stradbroke Island to Fraser Island in deep sand. In our hot summers it's degrees cooler in there.' A second level of shade is provided by the lacy canopy of a large tree fern. Underneath

Medinilla magnifica, a rare native of the Philippines with gorgeous flowers like lanterns, thrives.

Paths lined with tea-tree mulch wind through the garden which is completely planted out in a tapestry of foliage. Special additions, such as the bromeliad commonly known as Spanish moss that cascades here from an antique birdcage, provide highlights.

Swathes of the South American anthurium drift through the beds, in flower for months. 'I can't bear to cut them for the house,' says Mary. 'Even up here they are unusual in a garden.'

There are several of the six species of the genus *Calocasia* spp., the elephants' ears, as well as species of calathea, a myriad of different markings on the lush foliage. A collection of bromeliads and cordylines such as 'Tricolor' and 'Sonny Mathews', with its red splashes on green, provide excitement; a wonderful begonia with heart-shaped leaves and tiny sedums edge the paths.

The tropical rhododendron also do well, including the scented 'Flamenco Dancer' with its golden flowers. In mid October different cultivars of *Hippeastrum* ('the one bulb we can grow here') are spectacular.

At the entrance to the garden are several special trees; the *Grevillea* 'Moonlight' is covered in large cream flowers for months. The powder puff tree, *Calliandra*, is planted for the birds and *Eucalyptus ptychocarpa* for its massive gumnuts. A *Brugmansia* is covered in apricot perfumed flowers every 10 weeks. Mary is also keen on the new grafted eucalypts, such as *Eucalyptus ficifolia* which are perfect for small gardens.

Mary's favourite time is late afternoon, when the sun is low and the light glows through the garden. She insists the garden is easy-care. 'It's just a matter of neatening up,' she says. 'The only weeding I have to do is caused by birds dropping seeds of things like umbrella trees.'

The garden is Mary Collyer's creative outlet. 'It's my art,' she says. 'I am happiest in the garden.'

Opposite: The bracts of the bromeliad *Orthophytum gurkenii* are brown striped with cream, but become plain grey when wet.

Above: Anthurium drift through the beds.

Left: Begonias form a lush ground cover.

How this garden works

* Anthurium are very shallow rooted and need to be well-mulched. Mary Collyer cuts off spent flowers and trims dead leaves.

* The tropical rhododendron must have good drainage. 'They'll die if water sits around their roots,' says Mary.

* Mary fertilises in mid winter with blood and bone and sulphate of potash in a 5:1 ratio. Fifty kilograms is used on the 24 perch block. At the end of August, 80 kilograms of a mix of feather and fish meal, poultry manure, blood and bone and composted seaweed is used.

Wisteria magic

If daphne is the scent to enliven winter in a cold climate, surely the scent of Sydney must be of the common jasmine. While denigrated as a weed by many—and it is certainly a nightmare to control if one is not very strict—there is no fragrance more delicious than that of *Jasminum polyanthum*, which pervades the air in the harbour city during September. If the scent of the bull bay magnolia spells summer, and gardenias say Christmas, a sprig of jasmine in a lapel most definitely indicates that the cold and wet months of winter are over.

Each season of the year brings with it a particular fragrance. Simply watering the garden in the early mornings in spring, before the onset of daylight saving, is a unique and special joy, as the air in these few weeks seems to hold all the promises of the months ahead.

The common jasmine, trained in a single strand up a fence and then allowed to run along the top, to explode just once a year in a confetti of pink and white, makes a wonderful surprise when grown above a sedate hedge. The Chinese star jasmine (*Trachelospermum jasminoides*) can be clipped to within an inch of its life: it's popular in small city gardens, trained in diamonds and squares on rendered and limewashed walls. It is equally fabulous covering a wall or fence, simply allowed to romp through chicken wire and cut back with the hedge shears just once a year, after flowering.

Wisteria, which has been filling sub-tropical gardens with fragrance in the last few weeks, but is still to flower in the cooler areas, also needs a very definite regime. Hairdresser Lloyd Lomas and his wife Tricia inherited a 30-year-old wisteria when they bought their Sydney house; plaited and trained up stone columns, and along iron railings, it bursts into a wall of scented lilac racemes each September.

The wisteria in the Lomas garden benefits from a firm hand and regular timetable of maintenance and care. It is kept in check by pulling off all long shoots as they appear throughout the growing season, and by a further pruning at the end of summer, taking the plant back to the position where the flowers will form the following spring. No pruning is carried out in winter, except to tidy any stray shoots.

The Lomas garden is designed to be maintenance free. 'I don't let the garden get too demanding. I want to enjoy it; not have it rule me,' says Lloyd. 'And the garden echoes the different seasons as most things lose their leaves in winter, so the garden provides a changing background for the house. I love being able to notice the seasons, and there is always something flowering and scenting the garden. But I like fairly uniform colours and simple design and structure.'

Left: This 30-year old wisteria is trained up stone columns and iron railings.

How this garden works

* Lloyd Lomas would never recommend plaiting the stems of the wisteria. Although this looks terrific, he believes it weakens the trunk of the plant, allowing in moisture where the stems cross, and leading to disease. He feeds the wisteria twice a year, after flowering and at the end of autumn. Holes are made in the ground 2 metres out from the base of each plant; these are filled with Dynamic Lifter and watered in well.

Wisteria and wine

You understand why the Perth garden that Bill and Sandra Pannell have created over 10 years is so successful when you drink their wine. The Pannells were among the pioneers of the Margaret River area south of Perth, creating the acclaimed Moss Wood winery in 1969. In the early 1990s, and after selling Moss Wood, they bought into the Pemberton area, a four-hour drive south of Perth, and their elegant 'Picardy' wines are now eagerly sought.

Back in Perth, their house is cleverly designed as a series of rooms positioned to capture cooling summer breezes. 'The courtyard was planned by Bill so that the lounge room and the courtyard become one, and we can bring the outside inside,' says Sandra. An almost solid roof is formed over the courtyard by a perfectly pruned wisteria, a profusion of scented lilac racemes in late August and early September, and a canopy of cool green throughout searing summers.

'Because of the vineyard, Bill understands pruning,' says Sandra. 'But we found that when we grew one long stem, as in a vineyard, the wisteria didn't flower well. We found the plant performed better when we allowed two or three stems to form. Invasive roots haven't been a problem; by restricting the canopy, the roots are being controlled.'

'We first planted the courtyard with ferns and tree ferns, which was most attractive, but didn't suit the very structured design of the space,' Sandra continues. 'They were replaced with gardenias and lavender hedges, which looked beautiful for about four years, until the lavender started to go woody.' Now the white azalea 'Alaska' is most happy in the cool environment and is restrained by box hedges, propagated by Bill.

Bill's experience as a winemaker is evident in his garden, where he applies the same principles as in the vineyard. Everything is done with care; weeds are restricted, sprays used as little as possible, but are used at just the right time.

The Pannells chose the Pemberton region for their next vineyard partly because of the cold, but frost-free, climate. 'We loved the gardening we could do there,' says Sandra, 'and friends from Burgundy were amazed at the intensity of the flavours from some of the older vines already in the area.'

The soil is gravelly loam with a neutral pH of 6.5 to a metre, then is clay, but is free draining, even though the district enjoys a rainfall of some 40 inches per year. To prevent high vigour, no irrigation is used. 'We keep crop levels down to about 7 tonnes per hectare,' Sandra says.

The vines are trained low and excellent bunch exposure is achieved by a combination of careful shoot positioning and leaf plucking.

As in the garden, everything at the Picardy vineyard is carried out by hand; in the winery the ferments are hand plunged, to ensure that the tannins, so necessary for character, are soft. Pruning, leaf plucking and the picking is carried out by hand. The result is that, as in a much-loved garden, each vine is manicured.

Below: An almost solid roof is formed over the courtyard by a perfectly pruned wisteria.

Trevor Nottle's garden

While most gardeners are enjoying welcome spring colour and bracing for the summer that follows, bringing lots of hard work, Adelaide writer Trevor Nottle can think—just perhaps—about taking a break. He describes his garden, Walnut Hill, as a winter garden.

Named for the walnut trees that were planted about 1880, around an 1850s house of Mount Lofty sandstone, this garden is designed with the weather patterns in mind, and relies on autumn, winter and spring flowering plants. In summer, when heavy watering would be needed, the garden becomes dormant. 'I don't struggle with what's not appropriate; there are lots of things that will grow happily if you look at the natural habitat,' says Trevor.

The winter flowering bulbs from South Africa, China and Europe—crocus, cyclamen, babianas, sparaxis and gladiolus—are the stars at Walnut Hill. 'In the main, they are ones that come from areas where it also rains in winter, and we encourage them to naturalise,' he explains.

Along with the euphorbias for winter, there are many of the new grasses, which are left through the cold months to contribute form to the garden. There are also the artemisias, including *Artemisia* 'Powis Castle' and *A.* 'Lambrook Silver', to add to the winter story. In one corner of the garden *Euphorbia wulfenii* flourishes, along with the hardy species roses, in yellow and white, and a golden gleditsia. 'They all work in the winter and the spring, and then there is just the evergreen foliage to carry on through the summer.' Close by, the giant honeysuckle from Burma, *Lonicera hildebrandiana*, with enormous, dark yellow, heavily-scented flowers, romps to the top of a host tree.

Excitement in early summer is provided by the species peonies from Greece, the Mediterranean and China. Their strong root systems mean that they too are drought tolerant. 'They have fantastic flowers, don't need much water once they are established, and are not difficult to grow. But they hate competition from tree roots and need lots of sunlight to ripen the wood.'

Summer at Walnut Hill also sees the clematis star. *Clematis viticella* the small-flowered clematis from Spain and Portugal, flower in strong purples and blues, burgundies and pinks, and are very hardy. There are also varieties of *C. texensis*, summer flowering and from the south-west of the United States.

In the perennial border, the water-wise geums, day lilies and the iris are in flower, along with *Lobelia tupa*, from South America. A collection of sedums, all German hybrids, add excitement; there is 'Hester', which has burgundy foliage and musky pink flowers; there is 'Sunset Cloud', with dark crimson flowers; there is the purple leaved 'Bertram Anderson', along with 'Purple Emperor', with its foliage and flowers of burgundy.

Summer colour also comes from pots of lilies, orchids and succulents, near to the house where they can be nurtured. Hostas are grown in pots as they require too much water in summer to be planted throughout the garden. One of the stars is *Hosta* 'Sum and Substance' with enormous lime-to-yellow leaves. 'And we have amusing pottery and sculpture that keeps colour happening through summer,' says Trevor.

Opposite: At the base of a dead *Pinus radiata* is the fungus *Pholiota spectabilis*.

Below: *Heliotropium arborescens* 'Lord Roberts'.

Bottom left: Behind *Agapanthus africanus* 'Aureovittatuis', *Euphorbia characias* sub-species *wulfenii* is backed with *Yucca gloriosa* 'Variegata'.

How this garden works

* Trevor Nottle cuts most hellebores back in autumn; evergreen ones like *H. foetidus* are cut after flowering to avoid seeding.

* Tree peonies are cut back at the end of summer. Trevor then feeds with pelletised chicken manure.

Highland fling

In Dean Havelberg's Southern Highlands garden a background of different greens provides the canvas on which to paint rare bulbs and alpine treasures. Green is the colour Dean Havelberg relies upon in summer, when his first love, the bulbs, are over. 'Green on green, in fact', he says.

In this garden there are the bright, new greens of spring; the grey-greens of conifers such as *Cedrus atlantica* 'Glauca'; the forest greens and black-greens. In winter, the essential green of the conifers gives much needed structure to an otherwise bare garden.

While Dean describes his garden as informal, clipped hedges bring the various components together, so that the garden is a cohesive unit, throughout the year. Restraint and discipline of design contribute in no small way. Hedges are clipped after spring, once the new leaves emerge. A light 'haircut' is given in mid summer to keep the plantings dense.

Hillview is designed around circles and curves. Near the entrance is a small pool which rather sets the tone for the garden's style and appeal. Dappled light is created by maples and a white wisteria which bend over the pool. Several severely clipped cones of variegated box (*Buxus sempervirens* 'Variegata') lighten the scene. Swathes of the American skunk cabbage (*Lysichiton americanus*) appear from the pond, while around its edges, plants and bulbs grown from seed include *Helleborus niger* and *Galanthus* and *Erythronium*. There is also the much-talked about *Corydalis flexuosa*, which Irish plantswoman and writer, Helen Dillon, has described as 'the plant of the decade'.

Walking further into the garden, you arrive at a mature Himalayan cedar (*Cedrus deodara*). Planted beneath is a tapestry of shapes, textures and shades of green, created by massed *Hosta*, *Helleborus* and massed

Behind the alpine terraces, a copse of silver birch, underplanted with bluebells, leads to two deep-green cones of clipped conifer, dominating the entrance to the terrace by the house. Here, a charming rill is encased by a double border of box. A fountain at one end provides the restful sound of running water. Fish keep the rill clean and maintenance free.

The wisteria walk, glorious in spring, leads to the orchard, underplanted with narcissus, and to the large vegetable garden, which is rather more labour intensive! Soil preparation is the key to good vegetables and a complete fertiliser and compost are dug in a week before planting. Rather than being arranged in an intricate 'parterre', vegetables at Hillview are grown in rows to ensure that weeding is carried out as quickly as possible. Drama and glamour are added in mid summer when great swathes of *Lilium auratum* show off!

Opposite: Clipped cones of variegated box lighten a shaded rock pool.

Left: The water garden by the front terrace.

Below: The mature cedar towers over the terraced alpine beds.

oak-leaved hydrangea (*H. quercifolia*) with its white panicles adding light to the dark. This area is formalised by a half-circle of clipped box; each end of the hedge is accentuated by triangles of variegated box.

Nearby are the terraced alpine beds, the first area of the garden created, nearly 20 years ago. Among the collections here are sedums, the precious and temperamental *Roscoea*, and several varieties of *Rhodohypoxis baurii*, the South African bulb so suited to the Australian climate. There are also *Fritillaria*, particularly the delicate *F. acmopetala*, which Dean finds the easiest, and most readily available. There are species tulips, and several dwarf species daphnes, which can be very difficult to grow. These collections are grown in full sun in a mix of soil, sand and gravel to ensure excellent drainage. Beds are raised, for drainage, and so that some of the tiny treasures can be well appreciated.

Many of the special plants at Hillview are raised from seed sent by the various alpine societies to which Dean belongs. His main interest is in bulbs which can take between two and seven years to flower. Seeds, raised in a light, free-draining mix in polystyrene boxes, are planted in autumn to receive an essential chilling during winter.

Dean believes that water in a garden is very important, providing coolness and tranquility in summer and added interest in winter.

Blooming good ideas

Sue and Warwick Forge are passionate gardeners who have been lucky enough, and clever enough, to turn their love of gardening into work that they can look forward to every day. The fact that they run their horticultural book business from beautifully restored stables behind their *circa* 1888 house, Friesia, must add enormously to the pleasure.

The Forges run Bloomings Books, wholesalers and publishers of horticultural books, as well as The Green Book Company, which mail-orders retail garden books. Their Victorian house, in one of Melbourne's prettiest and greenest suburbs, was built in the Italianate style by the German architect John Bernard Koch for William Braha, the Consul to Victoria for Germany and Prussia. The garden was created when the house was built, it is thought with input from Baron Ferdinand Von Mueller, the first director of Melbourne's Botanic Gardens, who was a pallbearer at Braha's funeral.

'The front garden is very formal, very organised and symmetrical,' says Sue. A parterre of box hedging envelopes the generous and versatile euphorbias; *Euphorbia characias* subsp. *wulfenii*, with its blue-green leaves and acid-green flower heads, thrives in the cream-coloured gravel screenings from the Victorian country town of Yea. Cream cordylines on either side of the parterre are original and the nineteenth century plantings of yuccas, cannas and the palm, *Butia capitata*, make strong architectural statements. Close by, the easy-going *Euphorbia amygdaloides* var. *robbiae* grows in dry shade under trees, flowering for three months throughout spring. (She was brought into cultivation by an intrepid Englishwoman, Mrs Rob who, travelling in Turkey at the turn of the century, brought a piece home to England in her hatbox; the euphorbia became known as Mrs Rob's Bonnet.)

The kitchen opens onto a formal gravelled terrace. Classic lines are emphasised by a hedge of allardii lavender (*Lavandula* x *allardii*) along one side, which is clipped constantly. 'It was pruned from day one,' says Sue. 'That creates the strong structure at the base. If you let it flower it becomes much looser.' Facing is a hedge of Tahitian lime, which hides a suburban fence and is underplanted with blue and yellow iris—both cope well in dry conditions. At one end of the terrace, the evergreen *Arbutus* x *andrachnoides*, with its fabulous cinnamon-coloured bark and early winter flowers, provides an elegant feature.

Left: The gardens of the Italianate house, Friesia.

Peggy Shaw's garden

You can tell that Peggy Shaw is an artist the moment you push open her garden gate. Her garden, which is in the central Victorian town of Castlemaine, is terraced on three levels down a north-facing slope, and offers several lessons in colour and arrangement.

A trellis of the white climbing rose 'Mme Alfred Carriere' hides most of the garden from the road. The different areas of the garden are linked with arches of the climbing roses, the cream-coloured tea rose 'Sombreuil', so suited to the dry climate, and 'Clair Matin' with great trusses of pink and cream flowers, bred by French rosarian, Meilland, in 1960. 'I paint in watercolour and planned the garden as I would paint a picture,' says Peggy. 'Old roses and iris are among my favourite subjects.'

As you walk up Peggy Shaw's front drive you pass large beds of bearded iris in shades of blue, wonderfully combined with the aqua-blue of the South African *Ixia* 'Viridiflora'. (In nurseries, take care to look for the black 'eye' at the centre of the flower to ensure you are buying the true *Ixia* 'Viridiflora'.) In front of the house a bed of bearded iris is arranged, in a harmony of colour from blue to pink to magenta to lilac, to pale lemon, lilac again, and back to blues and magenta. The entire bed is backed by a stunning display put on by the copper-pink 'Mme Gregoire Staechlin', the climbing rose which does so well in the hot and dry climate of Castlemaine. This rose also looks superb when underplanted with bearded iris in shades of pinks and burgundies. 'Lady Marilyn' is the colour of crushed mulberries, and 'Loyalist' is the colour of a thick red wine. Both are tall, late flowering bearded iris which will hide the unsightly 'legs' of the climbing rose, flowering at the same time.

The bearded iris is, at first glance, perhaps a little flamboyant, but the flower is possessed with a delicate scent that is the harbinger of summer. The colour range is extraordinary; there are blacks through to true blues to lilacs, there are pinks and maroons and browns through to yellows. A brown iris such as 'High Roller' or the darker 'Rustler' looks wonderfully unpredictable, planted under the coffee-pink rose 'Julia's Rose'. This rose is said to be difficult, but it's worth putting up with her tantrums for her blooms of fragile coffee-coloured silk.

Above: A stunning display of the rose 'Mme Gregoire Staechlin'.

Glenrock

Sometimes we dismiss Mediterranean plants as being dull, without the depth of colour we feel we need to cool us down during the long Australian summers. There is nothing dry or boring about the Mediterranean plants at Glenrock, the terraced garden of Carolyn and Peter Robinson, on the Northern Tablelands of New South Wales.

As you drive into Tenterfield, massive granite boulders rise either side, toning perfectly with the glaucous leaves of the eucalypts, and you are reminded of early Australian paintings. This is Thunderbolt country; where bushrangers once galloped down the dangerous hills.

The soil at Glenrock is granite sands over clay; mushroom compost is used, and garden beds are built up to ensure good drainage. The perennial borders are cut back throughout the year and the clippings thrown into the 'chook yard'. 'It all comes out in six months as beautiful soil,' says Peter.

Paddock grasses, cut and baled at the end of winter when frosts and winds have removed any seeds, are used as mulch. According to Carolyn, 'Autumn leaves, particularly from the oaks, also make a great mulch. We mulch after the last winter frost because mulch holds the soil warmth in, thus increasing the severity of surface frosts. Our dry stone walls, on the other hand, protect against the frost, as a heat bank builds up during the day and is released at night.'

Hedges are very important as windbreaks in this very Australian landscape, but are kept at chest height to preserve views. Gaps are created at appropriate outlooks. A 'secret' garden is surrounded with a hedge of the Leyland cypress, x *Cupressocyparis leylandii* 'Leighton's Green'. This is tip pruned from the time of planting, 'topped' at 3 metres, and pruned three times a year to keep it dense. Separating this

Near the house and under a *Eucalyptus amplifolia* a large wooden deck has been built to look out across the lagoon. Dianthus has formed a soft carpet, making itself at home in the cracks between the weathered planks. The terrace beneath holds a mass of the roses 'Nozomi' and 'Immensee', recommended for holding a bank together.

Grasses such as *Carex* and *Miscanthus* are planted throughout the garden beds. 'They are rich green in summer and turn fiery colours in autumn. They rustle in winter and provide movement. We cut them back towards the end of winter, after they've added some height to the winter borders.' Carolyn absolutely adores the grey foliage of the cardoons and artemisias.

A new project is a herb and vegetable garden; the focal point is an arch of persimmon, wonderful in autumn when the fruit hang like golden globes. Stone paths dissect the garden and facilitate weeding. Hedges here are of privet (*Ligustrum ovalifolium*) which is frost hardy, copes with the summer heat and is faster growing than the more traditional box.

Opposite: Gentle blues, greys and greens cover the terraced beds at Glenrock.

Left: *Euphorbia myrsinites* massed behind *Sempervivum* 'Magnificum'.

Below: The acid-yellow flowers of *Euphorbia myrsinites* liven up in winter.

area from the house is a simple wire fence along which honeysuckle has grown thickly to form a scented hedge, creating a protective microclimate in which the plants thrive.

The multi-stemmed dogwood *Cornus amomum*, with its bright red stems, makes a great hedge of winter interest and hedges of the grey-leafed *Teucrium fruticans* edge some of the beds. Carolyn advises to 'create the bones of a garden first'.

The dry stone walls in the garden have been built by Carolyn with stone collected from the surrounding paddocks. In the stone-edged terracing, which takes the garden down to the lagoon, the blues and grey-greens of dianthus groundcovers thrive in gravel, along with thymes and succulents. The mid green leaves of *Euphorbia myrsinites*, with its acid yellow flowers to liven up winter, tone with the blue-green leaves of *Euphorbia characias* subsp. *wulfenii*. The rock roses, *Helianthemum* and *Cistus* do well on dry banks, and look good throughout winter.

'*Sedum* 'Autumn Joy' is a valuable plant as it goes through various stages of growth,' says Carolyn. 'The foliage is beautiful in spring and early summer and the flowers change from green to white to pale pink to dark pink to a rusty colour. It masses out quite well but is not invasive.'

Heronswood

Clive and Penny Blazey's garden, Heronswood, on Victoria's Mornington Peninsula, is set around a *circa* 1864 house and is something of a mecca for garden lovers. There is much to learn, for although Heronswood has the feel of a lush English garden of dense green colours, the Blazeys have long been advocates of plants which survive and flourish with sensible water use.

Two of the buildings at Heronswood are on the Register of the National Estate and from here the Blazeys run the Digger's Club, issuing regular newsletters and plant lists to members. In May 1996 the Blazeys bought the treasured 'goldfields' garden, The Garden of St Erth, created by well-known educator and garden writer, Tom Garnett and his wife

Penelope. This has allowed Digger's to expand the range of cold climate bulbs, shrubs and perennials that thrive in a climate very different from the maritime gentleness of the Mornington Peninsula.

When Heronswood opens to the general public every year, during Melbourne Cup Week, the enviable vegetable garden is at its peak. This is laid out in the style of a round parterre. Each of the eight beds is separated by a grass path; the area is divided from the next 'garden room' by ornamental lattice which supports climbing vegetables.

Heronswood demonstrates that productive gardens don't have to be boring. According to Clive Blazey, 'Most vegetable gardens are just straight rows, where no-one gives thought to the arrangement of leaves and textures. Ours is definitely decorative; it's certainly not designed solely for production. At Heronswood, the decorative vegetables and groundcover edibles are planted at the front and in the middle of each segment. Taller vegetables such as tomatoes—with some sunflowers thrown in—are at the back.'

Clever use of trellis isolates the decorative vegetable garden and allows essential but untidy vegetables to be kept somewhat out of sight. 'Shapeless vegetables, such as the melons, have to be grown in their own area, separated from the specific design, but as part of the overall design,' says Clive.

An integral part of the plan is the use of lettuces of many colours, shapes and textures. 'In summer it's not so easy as the lettuce tends to run to seed. If you want something that looks wonderful for a long time you've got to use different foliage like parsley and cabbages, and add the colour of, say, peppers. We also use a wonderful coloured Italian kale as well as five-colour silverbeet which also has beautiful textures,' he says.

Of course, you don't have to own hectares to create a productive and decorative vegetable garden. A little lateral thinking will turn the tiniest city plot or balcony into a salad basket or vegetable bowl. Edge garden beds with parsley, or red lettuce, instead of—or as well as—the more obvious *Buxus*. Underplant shrubs with the perpetual lettuce, use your boundary fence to support tomatoes or espalier fruit trees. Pots (or even strong plastic bags) can support a simple trellis of peas or tomatoes, a palette of lettuce or a collection of herbs.

It's been said before but, like all clichés, it's true—there is nothing like eating your own produce. All that is stopping you gathering your own meal each night is your imagination.

Opposite and below: The beautiful vegetable garden at Heronswood.

Left: Heronswood was built around 1864 and is a mecca for garden lovers.

How this garden works

* Soil preparation is everything with vegetables. Dig in gypsum and aged manure at least a fortnight before planting.

* Raise seeds around Easter to plant out for spring and summer bounty. In cool climate gardens, yellow tulips planted between light green lettuce and pink tulips between red lettuce look stunning.

The organic garden

In the town of Margaret River, in southern Western Australia, is a community garden called, until recently, The Organic Garden, now known simply as The Garden. Created and run by members of the Margaret River Alternative Technology Centre, the garden was established in 1989 to explore the methods of organic gardening and permaculture.

Created as a series of eclectic garden areas by the various personalities who run it, the garden provides something for everyone. Says artist Bec Juniper, 'For me the garden is a meeting place where people grow in creativity. There is a great harmony between people as they work together. It comes from the expression of ideas in actions, rather than constant talk.'

One founder of this exciting project, Shelley Cullen, talks of the philosophy of The Garden. 'Bringing community gardens into the public profile is so important,' she says.

The first area to be created, the 'home garden', is a mix of permaculture and companion planting. Throughout the garden, the culinary, medicinal and dyers' use of herbs is demonstrated. There is an Asian garden, housing symbolic and useful plants. A Japanese pine, a symbol of long life, thrives, and a peach tree represents good health and happiness. The ground is set with stones, for solidarity; tea is produced from a *Camellia sinensis* which came to the garden as a cutting.

At the centre of The Garden is a walled space, a memorial to one of its founders, Eva Dexter, who was instrumental in the organic movement in the area. Her much-loved purple and white irises and red roses are planted in the walled space; the area also houses Shelley Cullen's painting *The Lady of the Garden*. 'She symbolises gardening and children worldwide,' says Shelley.

Building with rammed earth, which is now an integral part of the Margaret River vernacular architecture, is also important in The Garden. An earthscape wall has been created with different types of sand and gravel by volunteers led by artist Lynne Tinely, who pioneered rammed earth art. The wall forms the backdrop to the outdoor amphitheatre, where local productions are staged.

Shelley Cullen perhaps sums up the spirit of The Garden when she describes 'the importance of creating beauty, a lovely space next to the school, a balance between utility and aesthetics. And since there have always been artists in the ongoing core group of gardeners, there has been a process of slow, creative evolution, where aesthetics are always a component of the garden design.'

Above: Step into a welcoming and verdant playground at The Garden.

Geelong Botanic Gardens

Geelong's magnificent Botanic Gardens, set on Victoria's Corio Bay, form a focal point in an easy-going and comfortable city that boasts a cosmopolitan restaurant and café-lined waterfront and promenade. The gardens were established in the 1850s, with Daniel Bunce as the first curator, from 1857 to 1872. (Bunce, a botanist and nurseryman, had also been an explorer, accompanying Dr Ludwig Leichhardt on his expedition to cross Australia, leaving from the important pastoral run, Jimbour House on Queensland's Darling Downs, on 10 December 1846.)

The Gardens now cover 4 hectares, next to a further 15 hectares of botanical parkland. Several of the trees in the gardens are listed on the Register of Significant Trees, including a massive *Sequoiadendron giganteum*, planted in 1873. There is also a perfect example of the Chilean wine palm (*Jubaea chilensis*), an endangered species, as it is used in Chile for making wine. (The tree is felled and the sap drained to ferment into wine.)

A maidenhair tree (*Gingko biloba*), planted in 1859, is now developing aerial roots, the only one outside Japan to do so. A fossil of a *Gingko*, 100 million years old, has been found at the foothills of the nearby Otway Ranges. The *Gingko*, by the way, is a tree of many uses. It is a marvellous garden tree for cooler climates, its beautifully shaped, delicate leaves providing golden autumn colour. The leaves also make a delicious herbal tea, and research into the *Gingko* as a drug against Alzheimer's disease continues.

Today, the visitor arrives first at a newer section of the Gardens through impressive, locally made iron gates. Here a mass planting of the glaucous *Echeveria* x *imbricata* is backed with the lime-coloured annual *Nicotiana*.

An exciting 40-metre perennial border forms the boundary between the 1960s extension and the historic part of the Gardens. The planting, managed and maintained by the Friends of the Gardens, runs from the hot colours of yellows and oranges at one end, through the spectrum of magentas and blues to, finally, creams and whites. Such fashionables as the pale orange *Trollius europaeus* lead into the vibrant *Penstemon* 'Firebird', the new *Angelica gigas*, producing rich red flowers on purple stems, the purple-flowered *Ledebouria cooperi*, with its chocolate-striped leaves, and into the blues of *Perovskia* 'Blue Spires' and *Eryngium* 'Blue Hills'—all toning with the subtle silver foliage of *Thalictrum aquilegiifolium*. The purple-leaved form of *Corydalis flexuosa* masses out in front,

along with the groundcover *Veronica gentianoides*. The border, which finishes with the white California tree poppy (*Romneya coulteri*), is renovated and divided in early spring and surplus plants are sold.

The Gardens also holds for the Ornamental Plants Collections Australia (OPCA) the collection of pelargoniums, which is housed in a purpose-built conservatory. 'We believe this is the only conservatory in the world that shows nothing but pelargoniums all year round,' says George Jones, one of the indispensable and generous Friends of the Gardens. 'Geelong is blessed with the perfect climate for the complete range of pelargoniums, without extremes of cold and none of the humidity they hate.'

Below: An endangered Chilean wine palm in the Geelong Botanic Gardens.

Hostas

The time of year when gardeners rush around their garden in joyful anticipation of each new leaf that unfurls as winter ends has certainly past, but the garden is still offering up a daily dose of excitement.

In cooler areas of the continent, the rhododendron continue to flower; the reds and pinks looking fabulous, picked when still in bud, and arranged with the purple leaved smoke bush, *Cotinus coggygria* 'Royal Purple'. The first flush of the tea rose 'Devoniensis' is with us, her clotted cream colours toning with the iris 'Lipstick Lies', and perhaps the most exciting of all roses, 'Mme Gregoire Staechelin' is giving her once-a-year-only performance. Her magnificent blooms sweep gracefully down, their striped pink and red buds matching perfectly the *Clematis* 'Red Corona' unfurling around her bare legs. And the hostas are covering the shady areas of the garden in a lush carpet of interwoven, textured foliage.

Hostas were first discovered by plant hunters in the Far East and were introduced to the West in the late eighteenth century. The Empress Josephine was one of the first European gardeners to fall in love with hostas, growing them at her house, Malmaison, just outside Paris.

The leaves of the hosta come in all sizes and almost all shapes, and a range of colours from bright lime-green to yellow, perfect for illuminating dark areas, through to greens and blues, to be laced into a border or to grace a courtyard. Then there are the fancy ones with splashes of colour in varying arrangements, to match with, and add dash and genius to, other plantings. A mass planting of *Hosta undulata*, its mid green leaves edged with cream, looks spectacular under the white lace-cap flowers of *Viburnum plicatum* 'Mariesii'. Writer Trevor Nottle recommends 'Antioch', with its green leaves with a creamy white edge,

for this spot. The hosta 'Ground Master' might be backed with the larger leaved *H. fortunei* 'Aureomarginata'; both are edged in yellow and echo perfectly the lemon tones in *Buxus microphylla*. These two look sensational growing with 'Aureomaculata' and the larger leaved 'June', where the placement of the colours is reversed, with the yellow splashed down the middle of the leaf.

Rob Cowell, who gardens at the inspirational Black Springs Bakery at Beechworth, loves *H. plantaginea* 'Grandiflora' because of its huge white perfumed trumpet flowers. 'It smells of gardenias and is tough,' says Rob. 'My granny has it in pots at Yarrawonga.'

Nicky Downer, arts consultant and passionate gardener, remembers hostas as part of her English childhood. 'They aren't easily grown on my windswept hillside here in South Australia,' she says. Her favourite is also 'Grandiflora', 'which is huge, 2 feet tall with clear green heart-shaped leaves. The best thing about hostas is the way the rain or dew collects in the leaves and creates an imaginary jewel.'

Trevor Nottle uses hostas as potted highlights in the water-wise summer garden. 'We have about 20 in tubs so they can grow into large clumps, as is their habit,' he says. Trevor's favourites include 'Sum and Substance', with its huge lime-green leaves and 'Gold Standard', which has large gold-centred leaves with a thin green edge, similar to another favourite 'Great Expectations'.

'These are tolerant of hot dry air, although they need regular watering and feeding and a dappled shady position,' he says.

Opposite: *Hosta fortunei* 'Aurea'.

Top left: *Hosta tokudama* 'Flavocircinalis'

Top right: *Hosta* 'June'.

How this garden works

* Most hostas enjoy deep rich fertile soil and high rainfall.

* Hostas are caviar to snails; once they find your hostas, the damage remains for the entire season. Put snail pellets in plastic milk bottles or cartons to attract snails but keep household animals safe. Wilmar Bouman, who gardens at Corinda, in the Hobart suburb of Glebe, nightly scours the garden by torchlight, after the first rains in early spring, with a bucket of hot water into which the snails are dropped.

* Divide hostas in spring, when new growth is appearing. Lift out the clump and divide, or simply cut off wedges with a sharp knife.

Tasmanian treasures

Sally Rigney assures us that she has created her garden by looking from the kitchen window while waiting for the kettle to boil.

Such a statement is way too modest, of course, and neglects to mention the years of love and devotion—and hard work—that have been lavished on this beautiful, and very individual, garden. The large garden, Delmont, in Tasmania's northern Midlands, has been created entirely by Sally, even to the building of the wonderful stone walls of local dolomite that provide so much of the character of the garden.

Sally has gardened at Delmont for 18 years, since she and her husband Allen took over the property from his parents. Then, the backbone of the garden was formed by just a few mature trees planted by Allen's

father. There were claret ash, the judas tree, with its cloud of brilliant pink flowers in spring, liquidambars, and a flowering cherry—greatly loved by the possums. 'My parents did the preliminary work,' says Allen, 'but, due to a lack of water, the garden could never be developed fully. Also, there was a line of wattles around the front of the house that were gross feeders and stopped anything else growing.'

Today water is pumped from the Macquarie River into a reservoir on the property. There is no shortage of water but, as in most country gardens, in summer the animals must come first.

Sally Rigney has designed the garden so that it is wonderful from inside the house looking out. It's not just good luck that everywhere you look there is a lovely vista. 'And the children helped build the walls,' she says.

For years, Sally collected stones from the paddocks. 'I carted three truckloads of rock a day. I never went out without my crowbar.' The walls are built wider at the base, for stability. 'And then I fit the stones together like a jigsaw … little stones also give stability.'

The heavy clay soil in the garden has been improved with the massive quantities of sheep manure that city people can only dream about. 'The soil is now full of earthworms,' she says. 'And I don't dig; I just mulch. If you mulch, you don't need to spend every day working in the garden. You do what you can, or what you enjoy.'

The visitor is greeted at Delmont by a drive edged with a sweep of stone walling that leads to the house and to beds of red floribunda roses, planted by Sally's mother-in-law, along with plantings of delphiniums.

Most areas in the garden house roses, a mixture of old fashioned roses, 'moderns' and David Austin. Sally is also fond of the easy-going rugosas, particularly the pink, repeat-flowering 'Sarah van Fleet'.

The vegetable garden is enclosed by hedges—of gooseberries at one end and of raspberries and blackcurrants at the other. The beds are divided into sections planted with seasonal kitchen needs.

Natural looking 'windows' are cut into the hedges throughout the garden to create vistas from inside the house—across the stone walls

and flat lawns to the orchard beyond. The orchard is about 30 years old and houses quince, a cherry, a plum, and several apple trees. 'We don't always get the fruit because of the possums and parrots,' says Sally. 'We go with the flow—if you get it you think 'this is great' and if you don't we wait for the next year.'

Opposite: Looking across to the flowerbeds from the stonewall-edged drive.

Below: Stone from the paddocks was used in the walls and steps.

Bottom left: Serene walkways and vistas.

How this garden works

* Sally Rigney says massive quantities of manure are the key to success with delphiniums.

* She has wrapped *Zincalume* around the trunks of trees that are particularly attractive to possums. The tin is secured with wire.

Adelaide's Botanic Garden

delaide's beautiful buildings and public parks, its up-to-the-minute bistros and restaurants, its glorious countryside and its wine growing regions, have all contributed to its atmosphere of a small but enlightened international city. The hot and dry climate of South Australia has also meant that Adelaide has become something of an international rose capital, the heart of the nation's $50 million rose industry.

The city's 41-hectare Botanic Garden is the setting for one of Australia's most successful public rose gardens. The centrepiece of the rose garden is a rare Colebrookdale fountain, imported from England in 1908. The surrounding, radiating rosebeds are backed with pillar roses, all underplanted with toning or contrasting iris. There is the elegant and repeat-flowering coral-coloured 'Lorraine Lee' bred in 1924 by the Victorian rosarian Alister Clark, underplanted with the delicately striped blue *Iris germanica* 'Terri Anne'. The 1963 Meilland rose 'Clair Matin', climbs above the massed iris 'Blue Shimmer' and 'New Moon', while the iris 'Winsome Lass' is teamed with the rose 'Fiesta Queen'.

The National Rose Trial Garden, the only such garden in the Southern Hemisphere, was opened in 1996, and is sited within the Adelaide Botanic Garden, close to the Rose Festival site. This important garden, where up to 120 new roses can be seen at any one time, is crucial in preventing new rose varieties being released onto the Australian market before being tested for suitability to our conditions.

'Now, breeders and producers from around the world can trial new varieties over a two year period, and have them assessed by a national panel of experts,' says Dr Brian Morely of the Adelaide Botanic Garden.

Adelaide's Botanic Garden opened in 1857. George William Francis, the first Curator, from 1855 to 1865, laid out the gardens in the style of the Royal Botanic Gardens at Kew in England, and was influenced by Versailles in France, and by the great Dutch and German gardens of the day. Entering the gardens from Adelaide's North Terrace through impressive cast iron Main Gates, made in Lambeth, London, and imported from England in 1880, the visitor passes a pair of Molossian hounds, replicas of those in the Vatican City. Further on is the Palm House, imported from Germany in 1857 and now fully restored; it is the only one of its kind in the world and features a display of Madagascan plants.

If you visit in late spring, don't miss the much-photographed twin wisteria arbours, each 64 metres long and of 12 different varieties of wisteria, an unforgettable sight when in full flight.

Above: A Colebrookdale fountain is at the centre of the rose garden.

Jan Waddington

The north-eastern region of Victoria is home to more than a fair share of talented artists. As well as craftsmen and women, chefs and winemakers, there are some marvellous gardeners. The approach to Jan Waddington's garden and nursery is along the Kiewa Valley Highway which snakes along the base of this beautiful valley. You drive between mountains which rise on either side; Mount Bogong in the near distance is peaked with snow from May to October. Above, the sky is a saturated blue.

Jan Waddington has to be a clever gardener. Her 1-hectare garden, set amidst a 300-hectare cattle property, copes with temperatures which range from the high forties in summer to −6°C in winter. In 1998, by early August, the garden had survived 30 consecutive nights of severe frost.

The beautiful structures throughout the garden are created by Jan's husband Rod, including the 30 metres of paling fence which provides some frost protection for the borders planted behind it.

Three giant red box (*Eucalyptus polyanthemos*) which tower over the garden also provide some frost protection, but are greedy for water and nutrients. Soil structure throughout the garden is good, but the onset of the October winds dries the soil. Jan's annual ritual of mulch and manure saves the garden from the summer drought, and ensures that perennial borders are packed with colour and foliage by early November, when Jan's annual weekend of garden lectures, rare plant sales, and good food, takes place.

The regime begins each spring with an application of cow or horse manure. 'In September we also mulch with a layer of, ideally, lucerne hay, expensive this year because of the drought. In autumn, we spread about 50 millimetres of mushroom compost on all the beds, except around camellias, azaleas and other acid-soil-loving treasures,' says Jan.

In the shaded beds Jan's collection of hellebores, invaluable for their flowers right throughout winter, thrive. '*Helleborus orientalis* comes in colours ranging from white to pink, mauve, deep plum and pale green. Some are spotted,' she says.

Among the first hellebores to flower is *H. foetidus* which, in early winter, is weighed down with great trusses of green bells. One of the varieties of this species, *H. foetidus* 'Wester Flisk', is very collectable, with its striking red stems. Jan finds this species will tolerate dry, poor soil. Both *H. lividus* and *H. argutifolius* (once called corsicus) have thick, toothed leaves and cream-green flowers which develop, and last, right throughout winter. Nothing looks so marvellous as the snow-white flowers of *H. niger*, which emerge in mid winter, pristine among the fallen red leaves of maples or liquidambar.

The salvias are great doers in any garden and fill out the sunny borders at Jan's. In her erudite but accessible *A Book of Salvias*, Californian botanist and horticulturalist Betsy Clebsch notes the sages are disease-resistant, often fragrant, and diverse in bloom, habit and colour. In Jan's garden '*Salvia wagneriana* flowers in winter with beautiful spikes of pink and white flowers. *Salvia cacaliaefolia*, with its lovely, succulent foliage and blue flowers, performs well in shade'.

Jan loves the iris for its blue-green leaves which provide accent in the border. 'The pale blue, frilly flowers of *Iris formosana* perform from late autumn to spring,' says Jan. '*Iris tectorum* does well in morning sun, and makes large clumps which can be left for many years.'

Below: Generous applications of mulch and manure ensures the perennials borders are vibrant and survive in cold weather.

Margaret magic

The oceans that lap Western Australia's Margaret River region on three sides provide a gentle climate, cooler than Perth just three hours to the north, but frost-free. The region runs from Cape Leeuwin, where the Indian and Southern Oceans meet, to Cape Naturaliste in the north.

Margaret River was a well-kept secret until recently, when its rich red wines burst onto the world market. Despite an influx of visitors, the community has been smart enough to recognise that its pristine, unspoiled beauty is an essential part of the area's appeal, while still providing travellers with the most up-to-the-minute hospitality. You can spend your days walking the karri forests, gazing upon azure-blue glass-clear waters, discovering rare orchids, or driving through dairy-rich country to wineries offering great food and luscious wines.

When Dr John Gladstones wrote his paper on the viability of Margaret River in the 1960s, he observed that the region was similar to Bordeaux, but with better winter rains. 'The Cape to Cape area is also one of the cleanest areas in the world,' says Shelley Cullen, daughter of Dr Kevin and Di Cullen, who helped pioneer the region to found the respected Cullen Wines. 'Fungal diseases are not a problem and, so far, sulphur sprays have been sufficient. People are very hesitant to use pesticides.'

The gentle nature of organic technology—the use of earth and stones for building—sits comfortably with the import of international money and methods. Many of the buildings in the area are of rammed earth. 'You will also find rammed limestone—it's lovely with pink oxides added. It's quite idiosyncratic to Margaret River,' says Shelley. 'This means that the area is also developing a vernacular architecture.' At the acclaimed Pierro winery, the second rammed-earth winery to be built in

In spring, the native wisteria, *Hardenbergia comptoniana*, grows through the red-flowered cockies' tongues, *Templetonia retusa* and the yellow-flowered *Hibbertia cuneiformis*. The south-western corner of Western Australia supports more than 100 species of the pea flowering family, Fabaceae, which Gabriel can identify by looking at the leaf alone.

There are also 'Cape to Cape' walks for the energetic, running from Cape Naturaliste to Cape Leeuwin, which is a mass of native daisies, the bush rose and tree hovea in spring. The walk will also reward you with some of the most wild and breathtaking coastline in the world; taking you past the heathlands leading to the savage Contos Cliff and Jewel Cave, one of the world's most beautiful limestone caves.

A fascinating interactive centre has been created on the site of the massive Lake Cave. The natural gardens around the centre are alive with south-west Australian indigenous plants. There is the pink and orange *Chorizema cordatum* and surely the most aptly-named plant of all, the ground-creeping *Kennedia prostrata*, nicknamed 'The Running Postman'.

Opposite: The Cullen Winery was a pioneer in the Margaret River region.

Left: The echiums add an architectural presence to the flower beds.

Below: *Chorizema cordatum*.

Margaret River—where glorious soft reds such as the just-released Pierro Pinot Noir 1997 are produced—Dr Mike Peterkin, like most of the winemakers in Margaret River, is moving closer to organic methods.

From September to November blue paper daisies edge the roadsides. In the Leeuwin Naturaliste National Park, species of orchids are still being discovered and walk trails have been created around where the orchids have been found. A guided walk with naturalist Gabriel Magyar, who knows where the different wildflowers appear at different times of the year, will reward you with snail orchids, green orchids, donkey orchids, spider orchids and the Bussell spider orchid.

'The *Leucopogon* was an important food source for Aborigines,' Gabriel points out. 'And the nice thing about the Epacridaceae family is that most produce small edible berries.'

Redlands

One of the many grand gardens in the Southern Highlands is Redlands, designed in the 1930s by the Danish-born designer Paul Sorensen, for Mr and Mrs Cedric Rouse. Rouse was an employee of Cecil Hoskins who, with his father, had established the iron and steel industry in New South Wales, and who was a patron of Paul Sorensen.

Sorensen arrived in Australia in 1915, soon establishing himself as a landscape artist. His biographer, the late Richard Ratcliffe, wrote of the landscaper's European influence: '... with these traditions he combined an original and individual style. His first principle was to take advantage of any existing site features, which, while not an unusual approach to contemporary design, was almost unknown when he began his career.'

The visitor to the several Sorensen gardens in New South Wales is struck by the sense of scale—the sweeping lawns with trees carefully placed—which was so much part of his design skill. It is also this understanding of the importance of space and balance that strikes the visitor when visiting the gardens of the Victorian designer, Edna Walling. While they obviously knew of each other, there is no record of these two designers ever meeting—and they worked mostly in different states. Richard Ratcliffe wrote that Sorensen, shortly before his death, said of his rival, 'Walling has left many words. I have left many gardens!'

Redlands, a 1.5-hectare, woodland style garden that displays Sorensen's skill at combining trees of extraordinary foliage and form, today is the setting for an important collection of mature, rare trees. The driveway is lined with the Sorensen signature, the purple-backed sycamore (*Acer pseudoplatanus* 'Atropurpureum') that tone with the copper beech (*Fagus sylvatica* 'Purpurea') planted closer to the house, and contrast with specimens of larch and hornbeam. The glaucous Blue Atlas Cedar (*Cedrus atlantica* 'Glauca') are planted behind deep-green foliage trees to increase the visual depth of the garden. Some trees were chosen because of the play of light on their foliage. According to Ratcliffe, one of Sorensen's most brilliant additions at Redlands was the ghostly foliage of a silver elm (*Ulmus procera* 'Variegata') which, surrounded by the dark foliage of the conifers, creates a spectacular 'shaft of light' effect.

Terraced on a north-easterly slope of Mount Gibraltar, Redlands is sheltered from winter winds and frosts, creating a unique, largely frost-free microclimate. Michele Scamps and her husband Dale Goodman, who bought the property in 1996, have undertaken a major renovation program while retaining the integrity of the garden. Mass plantings of camellias, rhododendron, dogwoods and magnolias have been added to Redlands' collection of cold climate plants. A new network of steps and pathways enables the visitor to explore the garden with ease.

Richard Ratcliffe would approve. Writing of Redlands in *Australia's Master Gardener—Paul Sorensen and his Gardens* he said, 'Although this garden has had several owners it has retained its initial form and shows Sorensens's intent completely. Being a garden constructed at an early stage of his career, the retention of its integrity makes Redlands an important example of Sorensen's work.'

Opposite: The garden at Redlands, in the Southern Highlands of New South Wales, was designed by Paul Sorenson in the 1930s.

Above: Space and scale—key features in a successful garden.

Left: A stone urn on a woodland path.

How this garden works

* The purple-backed sycamore, *Acer pseudoplatinus*, must be selected as small trees, as only 25 per cent grow true from seed with the desirable purple backs on leaves.

Avon Valley

Avon Valley Historical Rose Garden is set against the spectacular backdrop of Mount Bakewell, in the heart of the Avon Valley. If you're still confused by the story of the rose, a stroll around Avon Valley Historical Rose Garden will provide a rewarding lesson. The eight-year-old, 0.5 hectare garden houses a collection of roses which will take you on a trip through the somewhat confusing and complicated history of the genus; explaining the species; roses as they grow in the wild; as well as the different cultivated varieties.

Simon Faulkner's roses are set out chronologically, with explanatory plaques for each period displayed alongside each bed. They range from the wild species of each continent to roses of today; this is a history lesson which complements the historic nature of the town.

Many of us will understand when Simon confesses, 'I am going through a passionate romance with species and old tea roses.' His favourite roses include the sulphur yellow, globe-shaped *Rosa hemispherica* which performs as intended in drought and heat. There is the deep red, superbly scented 'Tuscany Superb', the moss rose 'Madame Hardy', with its distinctive green 'eye', and the glorious climbing 'Francis E. Lester' which you can often see in old country gardens, growing over stables and other outbuildings. Another favourite is the delicate pink 'Frühlingsmorgen', bred by German grower Kordes in 1942 from the *Pimpinellifolia* species.

The small specialist nursery at Avon Valley Historical Rose Garden specialises in hard-to-find roses, herbs and perennials. Simon grafts onto both *Rosa fortuneana* which produces nematode-resistant roses suited to the sandy soils of Perth, and onto *Rosa mannetii*, a good understock for roses to be grown in shallow soils.

One of the most interesting aspects of the garden is Simon's system of flood irrigation. 'This system allows us to water just twice a week in our summers of continuous heat, with temperatures which are often well over 40°C.'

From the top of each bed, the water main floods each channel, and fills a well around each rose. The water then moves on to the next rose. The herbs planted at the edge of each bed are watered by seepage as the main flow of water passes by. In this way, not a drop of water is wasted.

At Avon, rose beds are bordered by hedges of rosemary, lavender and the silver-leaved artemisia. Roses are underplanted with herbs—garlic chives and parsley—tough in a very demanding climate. The spectacular Californian tree poppy (*Romneya coulteri*) flowers from mid October to Christmas and self-seeding annuals have been allowed to make themselves at home throughout the garden.

Simon will strike a chord with many gardeners when he says, 'The garden is like a growing child as every day brings forth new character. It is through this that I feel rewarded and indeed privileged.'

Left: The rose 'Papa Meilland'.

How this garden works

* Simon Faulkner advises deep watering once or twice a week. 'Water in the morning so that roses are not damp overnight. Take care not to water the leaves which would encourage fungal diseases.'

Promised land

Wendy Roberts' Perth garden is something of a miracle. Started only two years ago, the garden, in spring, is a-wash with pinks, reds and golds as her roses flower. Every spare square of space is filled with roses; Wendy has not only covered walls and fences in climbing roses, but has taken over the airspace as structures have been built to accommodate and support more varieties that she simply cannot live without.

When you learn that Wendy has spent every day in the garden since she and her family moved into the house in the winter of 1997, and when you hear she is from a family of nurserymen, her success seems, perhaps, a little more understandable. 'Gardening is in my blood,' she says. 'My great great grandfather arrived in 1855 on the ship *Fortitude* to be head gardener at Government House in Tasmania.' Wendy's father still owns the respected Chandlers' nursery in Hobart's Sandy Bay.

In her Perth garden, Wendy inherited an important structure of limestone terraces and walls, already created by a local landscaper. She also inherited Perth's notorious sandy soil. 'I tested the bore water we were using to find it was incredibly salty. Then we tested the soil; it was so alkaline it was off the colour chart,' she says. 'So I had loads of soil taken out, and masses more brought in—and I've mulched and enriched. I don't like sheep manure as it can be very alkaline, and I try to alter the fertilisers rather than sticking with the same thing.'

In Wendy's garden, the existing collection of silver birch that was struggling in the Perth sand was replaced with roses. Iceberg roses were planted in the shaded areas, as well as the bright pink 'Zephirine Drouhin'.

Roses bred by the English breeder David Austin are afforded plenty of space. In this garden the long canes of 'Tamora', 'Evelyn' and 'Abraham Darby' are left so that the bush behaves like a climber. 'An expert came in for a week to prune them,' says Wendy. 'Instead of cutting the canes back hard, she left them to form great bushes.' One of the most beautiful David Austin roses is 'The Dark Lady'. 'The scent, and the size of the flower is extraordinary, and it holds its petals for so long, either on the bush or in a vase.'

Wendy is constantly looking at the garden as a picture and extolls its benefits. 'I think the garden gives so much back to you; it's so rewarding, so therapeutic, relaxing. It's good for the soul,' she says.

Above: Wendy Roberts' garden of roses and perennials.

Rose garden at Watervale

Hundreds of people make the annual pilgrimage to Walter Duncan's rose garden at Watervale, in the beautiful Clare Valley for his open day each November.

It's not just because the historic Hughes Park homestead, *circa* 1867, is so important, nor just because the 1 hectare rose garden is so beautiful. It is also because Walter Duncan is one of the characters of the gardening world and is so generous with his time and advice.

The homestead sits amidst 90-year-old trees behind wide beds of perennials—foxgloves, Canterbury bells, poppies, hollyhocks, daisies, iris, hellebores and catmint—which form underplantings to layers of roses of every description.

The Rose Garden at Watervale was started 20 years ago and is known for its heritage roses—the display garden contains about 700 varieties.

According to Walter Duncan, 'The scope for designing with the old-world roses is much wider than with the modern. There are different leaf forms, different flower forms, wonderful scent which evokes times past; you get leaf colour and fruit in autumn.' The range of old roses includes species roses—those growing as they were found in the wild—such as the popular rugosa, so suitable for hedges, through to the later cultivated groups of *Gallicas*, *Albas*, *Damasks* and *Centifolias*.

'Heritage roses lend themselves to open and free planting and are less regimented and more forgiving than modern roses,' says Walter

Duncan. 'Tuck them into the flower borders. I like to keep roses in groups—rugosas, Bourbons and Gallicas toward the front as they are shorter and mix into borders'.

This formal rose garden is divided into two 100-metre-long rose walks, shaded by rose-covered arches. The 1843 Bourbon rose 'Souvenir de la Malmaison' and 1872 Bourbon 'La Reine Victoria' grow together, the delicate shell-pink of the former toning wonderfully with the slightly deeper pink of the latter. The lower-growing 'La Reine Victoria' covers the 'legs' of 'Malmaison' which is more vigorous, covering the arch. On the next arch, 'Souvenir de la Malmaison' and climbing 'Duchesse de Brabant', a pink tea rose bred in France in 1857, grow together, extending the flowering season. Deep beds of roses and perennials flower on either side of the grass paths. 'Roses love other plants, particularly bulbous Spanish and Dutch iris', says Duncan. 'Companion plants and groundcovers like strawberries, campanulas and forget-me-nots also look completely at home.'

As well as arches in the garden, Walter Duncan is keen on poles and posts for form and height. Simple treated posts are suitable; he warns against using creosote posts as the oil mixes with the earth rendering it toxic to the nearby plants.

The climate of South Australia is perfect for roses, but summers can be extreme. Walter Duncan has protected the stems of his roses, which give essential height to the borders, by wrapping them in tea-tree bark!

Opposite left: 'Queen of Denmark'.

Opposite right: 'Mme Isaac Pereire'.

Below: 'Souvenir de la Malmaison'.

Bottom left: 'Zepherin Drouhin' with the *Clematis* 'The President'.

How this garden works

* Deep-water roses just once or twice a week and mulch heavily to preserve moisture and keep the soil cool. Roses don't mind being mulched right up to the stem; such treatment will encourage fungal diseases in most other plants.

* Plant more than one rose together to extend the flowering season. Clematis, which develops fascinating seed heads after flowering, looks wonderful planted with climbing roses. The *Clematis texensis* 'Gravetye Beauty' which flowers throughout summer, looks extraordinary planted together with the cream and pink Meilland-bred rose 'Pierre de Ronsard' which flowers from early summer to Easter. Try other combinations such as the late spring, once-only flowering rose 'Mme Gregoire Staechelin' with *Clematis texensis* 'Duchess of Albany', or the large flowered hybrid 'Fair Rosamund'. The clematis cover the bare legs of the roses!

* Clematis like to grow toward the sun, with their roots planted in shade. A visitor to my own garden passed on his advice for keeping clematis roots cool. Cut a piece of shade cloth in a circle. Make one slit to the centre, place around the fragile stem of the clematis, to preserve moisture, then cover with mulch.

View's End

Kaye Clancy and Lindsay Wright's rose garden is situated about 80 minutes from Melbourne, on the Bellarine Peninsula. With wonderful views over Port Phillip Bay in one direction and the You Yang Ranges in another, it is called, appropriately, View's End. It's also the combination of clever design, brilliant planting and superb maintenance that make this garden very special.

Roses feature at View's End. On either side of the entrance are standards of the rose 'Heidesommer' and the tea rose 'Archiduc Joseph'. Close by, *Clematis cirrhosa* var. *balearica*, which is smothered in cream-flecked-with-burgundy flowers, blooms from April through the winter months.

The pillars supporting the verandahs of the house are covered in roses, including 'Cornelia' and the deep cerise, wonderfully scented 'Mme Isaac Pereire'. The roses outside the bedrooms are chosen for their fragrance; there is dark, velvet-red, highly scented 'Guinee' as well as 'St Cecilia 'and 'Mme Alfred Carriere'.

Colour combinations play an essential part in this garden. In one of the several deep garden beds, the apricot-coloured rose 'Just Joey' tones with a backing of Chinese lantern (*Physalis alkekengi*) and an underplanting of nasturtium in the same colour. The native hibiscus *Alyogyne*

huegelii 'West Coast Gem' blooms in the same blue as the catmint that edges the bed. Other garden beds contain more clever plantings. A border of the cerise-coloured iris 'Lady Friend' tones with the purple-leaved *Berberis thunbergii* 'Atropurpurea' and bronze fennel, planted behind.

The exercise of colour layered upon colour is repeated nearby, with the cerise flowering broom 'Crimson King' and 'Lady Friend' backed with purple-flowered cherry pie (*Heliotrope* spp.). Down the centre of this bed are multiples of the rose, 'Moonlight'; while its blooms are white, to accompany a nearby planting of *Viburnum opulus*, its red stems are in tune with the broom and the iris.

View's End was designed to be water-wise. In the dry borders, under mature eucalypts, sea hollies, heucheras, catmint and mollis azaleas thrive. Oleanders, olives, sedums and succulents are also favourites.

The value of soil preparation and maintenance is very evident at View's End. Thirty-two trailer loads of seaweed from nearby Port Arlington are used, unwashed, in the garden, alternated yearly with lupin straw from the chookyard. 'We mulch continuously,' says Kaye.

Bottom left: View's End.

How this garden works

* In this garden clever signs are made by painting the name of a rose in green on the bottom of a can which has been painted cream. Holes are punched and wire used to secure the sign in the ground.

* 'Grey water', from the washing machine, dishwasher, etc. is used on the garden. No special detergents are used, and frogs and birdlife are abundant.

* A recipe for healthy roses from a country gardener: Fill half a 4-litre bucket with blood and bone, add 1 kilogram of sulphate of potash, mix, top up with more blood and bone, and mix. Give one or two handfuls to each rose, three to four weeks after pruning, again when the roses flower in the late spring, then in summer, and again before they flower in autumn.

Hill River Station

Hill River Station is a cattle and sheep property on the eastern slopes of the Clare Ranges in South Australia.

When the property was acquired in 1876 by the present owner's great grandfather, John Howard Angas, a massive tree planting program was instigated to provide shelter for the stock; a mixture of local gums, kurrajongs, pines and olives was planted. The olive trees, which provide feed for the stock, regenerate after fire, explains owner, Alastair Angas. Hill River Station is one of a handful of properties in Australia to breed Sussex cattle. 'They're an old English breed; very docile,' says Angas. 'We've been breeding them for 30 years now. They are very popular in South Africa and Zimbabwe, so we felt they would have a place in a dryer, hotter climate in Australia as well.' They also breeds merinos.

One hundred and twenty-five years ago, the garden comprised an orchard, a citrus grove and a vegetable garden to supply the needs of the station. The young plantation trees were raised in the kitchen garden and watered with a 44-gallon drum.

The beautiful garden that exists today was laid out over stages, and greatly extended in the 1920s by Alastair Angas' mother. A sweeping drive lined with English oaks brings the visitor around the property and through a series of original station outbuildings. 'I planted a lot of those oaks,' says Angas. 'They're my contribution to posterity. They're quite fire resistant, not like pine trees who turn their toes up as soon as they smell smoke.'

The garden, which is on several levels, is set around a 150-year-old homestead; the slate for its roof came to South Australia from Wales as ballast. In front of the house are wide lawns leading down to the lower terrace, where the main rose garden is arranged as a massive square, divided into four large beds.

'My mother-in-law planted a whole bed of "Talisman",' says Janet Angas. This large-flowered, remontant tea rose has a pink striped bud, and opens to a gold and apricot bloom, with a beautiful scent. There are beds of the apricot 'Just Joey', the Australian-bred 'Lorraine Lee', 'Peace' and 'Queen Elizabeth', as well as the more modern, 'Pascali' and 'Gold Bunny'. The only feeding that is necessary at Hill River Station is an occasional dose of sheep manure from beneath the shearing shed. 'And lucerne is the best mulch you can possibly have,' says Janet Angas. 'It doesn't break down too quickly, puts nutrients back into the soil, doesn't blow away; it's a once-a-year job.'

'It's the stubble after the plant has matured and gone to seed,' explains Alastair Angas. 'The seed is taken off first, so that we don't have unwanted volunteers in the garden.' He adds, 'We now have an automatic watering system and that's the only reason I'm still alive.'

Near the house, the sides of the tennis court are covered in the luscious 1838 tea rose 'Devoniensis' which, in the rich Clare soil, is tipped with deep pink. She is very full, with a marvellous lemon scent, and has been flowering here for over 100 years.

Left: Hill River Station.

Courtyard magic

The work of the Sydney garden designer Gordon Sykes is as different as it is brilliant. Whether designing a large mountain garden or a tiny city garden, his work is successful, though never clichéd.

His experience and skill are again evident in his unique Sydney garden, which is made up of several contained, small areas, each completely individual.

Gordon and his wife Ann inherited the design and planting of his predecessor when he bought his property, on Sydney's North Shore, four years ago. Asked how a designer approaches a new project, he advises, 'Start by looking at the position of the house in relation to the garden. Ask what the garden is doing for the house.'

A tiny courtyard garden outside his dining room is now a lush rainforest area. A 'brook' of smooth white stones creates a meandering feeling, creating distance in a very small space. The windows of the dining room reach the floor, bringing the rainforest into the house. Verticals are created by a palm and a copse of sacred bamboo (*Nandina domes-tica*). A carpet of bromeliads creates a deep-green, cool, understorey. 'A lot of people don't like bromeliads,' adds Gordon. 'They see them as too exotic—but they have an architectural feel, a wonderful contrast in the foliage, and the flower lasts for months. They will grow in deep shade, they need little soil—important where the other plantings are greedy. They need little water—none at all in winter. They are very useful in a city garden—maybe in a narrow, dark, hard-to-reach area between two houses.'

'This is not an area which could be created on paper first,' says Gordon. 'I moved the plants around like pieces of furniture. In a very intimate area you have to feel your way.'

Perhaps the most important aspect of any garden, large or small, is the quality of the light. 'In this small courtyard, the light changes throughout the day, illuminating the garden differently, at different times. It's the way the light falls, through the stems and leaves, that creates the dimension of the garden and its special nature,' he says.

'Most clients won't expect you to talk about the value of light and what it's going to do in their garden,' he continues, 'but there is a direct connection between the success of the landscape and the shadow pattern in a garden.'

Gordon would recommend investing in one special, established tree. 'You will immediately achieve a pattern of light and movement through the boughs of the tree. A beautiful tree is a very good piece of garden furniture.'

The elements of design so important in a large garden—scale, movement and texture—can be used with great success in a small garden. 'Different textures and patterns in paving also prevent the eye from travelling the full length of the scene at once. Pattern keeps the eye

captured and holds the interest,' says Gordon. 'If you left the garden open all the way through, the eye has nothing to explore.' He adds, 'Don't make a definitive statement about a long narrow path. Stepping stones suggest there is something exciting around the corner.

'I first learnt in Japan that by decreasing the size of the stepping stones as you go away from you—for instance in a narrow space beside a city house—just marginally, you increase the sense of space. Similarly, in a flower border, you keep the darker colours close to you, the lighter colours further away.'

Even with small gardens you can use borrowed landscape-trees from another garden or a park across the road. 'Use blocks of similar foliage. Too many different textures and shades become confusing. The eye doesn't know what to look at. Small spaces don't have to be simplistic—neat box hedges—to work. If you make your garden very rigid in design, this extension of your own space won't be possible.'

Just as the natural light can be used to great effect, 'Lighting a garden for the evening will give a complete change of style,' says Gordon. 'At night you must be very selective to highlight certain areas and create a little bit of magic.'

Above all, his advice is to observe. 'Think about why a particular thing pleases you. Why does a texture make something look better than a flat surface, why does a colour make you feel warmer, why does a certain line in a garden make you feel more enveloped? Question—always.'

Opposite: Gordon Sykes's tiny courtyard garden, which includes *Aechmea fasciata*.

Left: *Aechmea fasciata* adds drama to any garden.

How this garden works

* Study the light in your garden—it's an important design tool.

* 'Less is more' in night lighting.

* Smaller stones and lighter colours in the distance will create a sense of space.

* Borrow your neighbours' landscape and plants to allow your eye to travel to it, rather than to stop at your boundary.

Dunedin

It's Annabel Scott's good 'gardenkeeping' that keeps Dunedin, a large and beautiful country garden surrounding an 1860s homestead in northern Tasmania, at its peak.

The beauty of the garden belies the fact that this part of Tasmania can be harsh gardening country. The soil is, in many parts, clay, and good ground preparation was crucial. Dunedin is a working sheep station, and great quantities of sheep manure have, over the years, broken down the once unworkable soil.

As in many country gardens, water is always an issue. What water is available is supplied by a spring on top of a hill on the property and water pressure is dubious. As well as a mulch of manure and mint and fennel trash, from the local essential oil factory, deep watering of each garden bed, once every 10 days, is the key. An essential hedge of *Cupressus macrocarpa*, which protects the garden from hot, drying winds, is also greedy for moisture and nutrients. Plants in this area of the garden need to be more water-efficient.

As well as bushfires during hot summers, the garden must cope with temperatures which drop to –5°C in winter. The vicissitudes of climate provide, for many gardeners, much of the joy. 'The garden is so exciting through each season,' says Annabel. 'One month there are just a few bulbs—crocus and galanthus—then the fritillarias come, then you might have some new leaves on a tree and then, in summer, colour.'

'Some beds are best in certain seasons and can be avoided in off-seasons,' says Annabel, 'and I'm ruthless with plants that sulk'. Another trick is to hide plant signs under rocks—apart from looking more attractive, birds find it harder to scratch the signs out of place!

Restraint is also very important, never more so than when choosing garden statuary. 'It's better to save for just a couple of beautiful pieces,' she advises.

Matching your collection of plants to the climate and conditions you've inherited is also her sensible advice, however. While Annabel loves the beautiful Himalayan poppy, *Meconopsis betonicifolia*, with which many of us persevere, she believes that is better left to her colleagues who garden in the mountain climate behind Hobart, which is more matched to the plant's natural environment.

Her advice for the new gardener is 'Don't rush in too quickly! Be patient. It's important when designing a garden not to try to do it all at once. I love drawing plans but I also like to let the garden evolve.'

I asked Annabel what makes a garden great. 'I don't know,' she replied. 'Love?'

Left: A statue of Pan is part of the garden's beautiful statuary.

Hollywood Reserve

Just 10 minutes from the centre of Perth is one of the city's best kept secrets—an inspirational 6.5-hectare park of Western Australian native plants with the somewhat unlikely name of the Hollywood Reserve. A stroll just off a suburban road will lead you to a variety of charming paths—and will remind you that nature, if left alone, will create a scene of simple beauty. Add the white flash of a cigarette packet, the glare of a soft drink can, and all is ruined.

In a great example of community and council cooperation, this area of bushland was declared an A-class Reserve in 1974 by the City of Nedlands Council. The reserve is maintained today by local residents and school children in association with the council.

The story of the fight for the declaration of the reserve is as moving as the area is now peaceful. Local resident, Bill Day, used to walk in the area with his daughter, identifying the wildflowers. After his young daughter died, Day scattered her ashes in the bushland she loved, planted more indigenous trees and shrubs, and started a petition to preserve the area.

Each year since the mid 1970s Nedlands Council has planted some 2000 native trees and shrubs in the reserve, many indigenous to the Nedlands area, others sourced from around Western Australia. A 1986 census of native plants in the reserve revealed that the area supports over 200 species, 71 of which are indigenous to the Karakatta sands of the reserve. Among the trees are eucalypts, casuarina and banksia; there are hakea, grevillea and kangaroo paw as well as orchids and verticordias. Many of the plants are marked and a fascinating natural history trail has been set out through the reserve.

Paths wind between the small-growing eucalypts *Eucalyptus tetragona*, *E. youngiana*, and *E. preissiana*, the bell-fruited malle, which was named after the early botanist, Preiss. There is the fabulous *Eucalyptus pyriformis* with its pear-shaped fruit and yellow flowers, growing with the pink-flowered *Melaleuca filiifolia*, the honey myrtle, both from the southwest of the state. Wattles such as *Acacia pulchella* grow with the Geraldton wax, *Chamelaucium uncinatum* 'Purple Pride'. The wild wisteria, *Hardenbergia comptoniana*, scrambles over the white-flowered *Grevillea vestita* and groundcovers include *Grevillea critmifolia*. Towering above is the original upper storey of jarrah, karri, marri, she-oaks and tuarts.

Local schools use the reserve for nature study and conduct weeding and planting days, while the Hollywood Primary School documents the flora, fauna and fungi of the area.

Birds that call the reserve home include the ring necked parrot, the tawny frogmouth and the boobook owl. Claire Welsh, whose charming wildflower garden is close by, says, 'Most birds are dependent on Australian plants for nectar, insects, shelter, nesting and travelling. The preservation of this close interdependence of fauna and flora is vital to areas such as this reserve, a dwindling resource in the suburbs.

'Every piece of urban bushland is vitally important,' she adds. 'We all need to work actively to reverse the loss of parkland to weeds and through lack of regeneration for various reasons.'

Below: *Eucalyptus pyriformis.*

Austin country

You need a certain courage to take your camera into Ray Joyce's domain. One of Australia's foremost photographers, Ray and his designer partner Elaine Rushbrooke have brought the artist's eye to the creation of their beautiful rose garden on the Huon River, south of Hobart.

Occupying an extraordinary site, on the banks of the glass-still river, this garden displays and represents David Austin roses in Tasmania. From his base in the north of England, Austin breeds roses which have old fashioned, voluptuous form and scent, but modern disease resistance and repeat flowering characteristics. His first rose, 'Constance Spry', bred in 1961 and named after the English flower arranger, is still, perhaps, his best known and most popular.

Some of Australia's most moving gardens have been created with an artist's sense of scale, balance and colour. The Scented Rose is no exception.

While Elaine and Ray took over a 100-year-old garden and inherited impressive clipped cypress spheres, as well as essential hedges, most of the garden is just three years old.

Like all good gardeners, they are generous with their advice. A crucial piece of information is that you should disinfect secateurs when pruning roses to prevent the spread of disease from one bush to the next. This caution stands when simply picking a bunch of roses, or when 'dead-heading'.

Just *when* you prune will depend upon where your garden is. In Sydney, I prune in early June, and then again, lightly, in August. My climbing 'Devoniensis' is never without a bloom. This rose grows over a front fence, and with its thorns prevents the metre reader from hoisting himself up and over the fence—not helpful to the beds of gardenias

That these owners are artists is evident at every turn. The garden is beautifully maintained, with no 'dead heads' or scrappy leaves to assault the artist's eye, nor spoil the photographer's frame. It's a good exercise to photograph your garden, not just for your records, but also because you are forced then to focus on, and evaluate, a small area of the garden. The eye, undistracted by all that is happening in the garden 'at large' will see design and maintenance faults very quickly.

At The Scented Rose, Elaine creates beautiful signs to name each rose. She paints wooden posts—20 millimetres by 20 millimetres and 1 metre high—in a dark green matt. With a flat ferrule number 2 brush, she paints the name of each rose, in white. Hammered in to a depth of 0.25 of a metre, it's hard for those frustrating birds to peck them out!

Opposite: December roses at The Scented Rose in Tasmania.

Left: Arches of roses and clematis direct the visitor through the garden.

Below: A mass of flowering pelargonium covers a shed.

below—instead of coming through the gate. In my Highlands garden I never prune until mid to late August, to ensure that flowering waits for my open weekends, 70 days later. In Tasmania, where log fires can still burn in December, Ray and Elaine prune in July. In Queensland, at Culpepper's rose garden and nursery, the roses are pruned in February, to allow the bush to rest in the hottest months of the year.

At the Scented Rose, there is plenty of interest when the roses are not at their peak. Favoured perennials for underplanting and companion planting include the white *Campanula persicifiolia*, *Dianthus* 'Doris', beautifully scented, particularly early in the morning and many of the species of geranium, such as the apple green *Geranium renardii*.

Clematis grow particularly well in this part of Tasmania; the true-blue hybrid 'Blue Boy', the cerise 'Madame Julia Correvon' and purple 'Vyvyan Pennell' grow over the archways, with the climbing roses.

Magical Malmsbury

As much of Australia swelters in summer, the 'hill station' areas of the country offer delicious evening respite from the debilitating daytime heat. In the Southern Highlands of New South Wales, swirling summer mists are among the district's many charms; you can need a log fire even on Christmas Day. The great gardens of the area are added attractions.

Malmsbury is one such garden, owned by Dr Jenny Learmont and Professor Ian Bickerton. Jenny has been awarded an honorary doctorate for community service for her work in mental health and HIV–AIDS. Ian is a professor in American history. It is not surprising that this is a somewhat intellectual garden, containing rare trees and unusual plants, but Malmsbury is also a garden to be enjoyed simply for its beauty.

Hedges, and copses of special trees, are used to create several enclosed, individual garden spaces, each with a unique feel, making the garden seem much larger than its 0.5 hectare. Balance is provided by plenty of lawn space.

The visitor arrives at Malmsbury in early spring to thousands of Monet tulips in tones of the palest pink through to carmine, planted with a mass of pink ranunculus. A collection of magnolia including M. 'Elizabeth', M. stellata 'Rosea' and M. liliifora 'Nigra' add a tracery of exotic branches followed by weeks of scented flowers. The picture is enclosed by a clipped hedge of Lonicera nitida which immediately contributes structure to the garden.

To the right of the entrance is a woodland planting backed, for privacy from the road, with a hedge of *Camellia sasanqua*. A tall edging of *Artemisia* 'Powis Castle' encloses a collection of silver birch underplanted with masses of daffodils.

Behind the house is a small 'herb court' of santolina, chamomile and thyme, planted between sandstone paving and formalised by a hedge of *Teucrium fruticans*. (The grey-leaved *Teucrium*, with its small blue flowers, was a favourite of the Victorian designer Edna Walling, although she would never have used it clipped.)

Even in the misty Southern Highlands' climate roses do well, particularly the climbers; in November, 'Mme Gregoire Staechelin' shows off, with a great display of frilly, pink, down-facing blooms covering a south facing wall. The cream tea rose 'Devoniensis' covers several posts along the drive. Behind a hedge of Allardii lavender is a mass planting of the pink hybrid tea rose 'Queen Elizabeth'; she is backed with trellises of wisteria.

Another 'secret garden' near the front door holds a collection of the Japanese maples of the Dissectum group, to ensure that this garden is fascinating throughout each season.

From the detailed planting close to the house a fastigiate tulip tree (*Liriodendron tulipifera* 'Fastigiatum') leads the visitor to an expanse of lawn which is backed with evergreen alders. Grass paths which lead behind all the beds again provide a sense of a much larger garden. In a far corner, a small water garden is hidden within hedges of box, protected by a horseshoe of golden robinia. A rill is set within a floor of scoria which forms a perfect bed for the creeping green of the pincushion plant, *Saxifraga* 'Apple Blossom'. A backing of the intensely-blue *Ajuga* 'Bugle Boy' contrasts with the yellow of the robinia.

Opposite: The drive at Malmsbury is edged with clipped *Lonicera nitida*.

Bottom left: Exotic trees spill over beautifully kept hedges.

Below: Thousands of tulips flower in spring at Malmsbury.

How this garden works

* After flowering is the time to hard-prune wisteria; then just pull away the soft shoots as they appear.

* The evergreen alder is most definitely not a tree for a city garden; they love water and are very fast growers.

* At Malmsbury, hedges are clipped fortnightly to keep them dense, providing the 'bones' of the garden. The grey-leaved *Artemisia* 'Powis Castle' should not be pruned until the risk of frost is well past.

* Tulips are not lifted at Malmsbury; add an organic fertiliser after the leaves have died down.

Look who's talking

All sorts of very sane people talk to their plants. I think they're sane, anyway. Perhaps that's because I talk to my plants. Doesn't everybody? You can't help loving plants, can you? After all, they don't 'talk back'. And plants don't stamp their feet, or slam doors. They don't put their clean clothes back in the laundry basket. Plants just keep giving, uncomplaining—without a 'it's not my job', or 'why is it always me?'

Autumn is perhaps the best time of all in the garden. While bountiful as you reap the edible rewards of your 'good gardenkeeping', it is also a season of inexplicable melancholy and mixed feelings. The autumn garden is so much more subtle than the exuberance of spring and the voluptuousness of summer. There is time to appreciate the turning colours and changing textures, time to plan for next year before the garden becomes bare.

Winter is never sad for a gardener, however. It is a season of self-satisfaction as you cut back, tidy and mulch as you 'put the garden to bed' for the chilly months. Excitement soon mounts as the blue-green tips of the spring bulbs start to push through the frozen, moss-covered soil. Last August in my garden, Rowandale, while winter-pruning the last of the roses, I looked down to see a patch of the tiny narcissus 'Tete a Tete', so bright and perky.

Blooming all through winter was *Camellia japonica* 'Nuccio's Gem'. Breathtakingly beautiful, yet so dignified. And 'Shiro-Chan'—just lovely, and oh, so restrained. She's definitely in the 'less is more' category. Which brings to mind the decorating of the Christmas tree. I suggested just tartan bows, while my children wanted the works, saying 'No, Mummy, more is more'.

When you see your plants in mid winter, bowed down by the cold, the green bells of *Helleborus lividus* sugar-coated with frost, you love them for their courage and say 'Brave soldiers'.

When spring arrives at Rowandale and the wisteria arbor is in full, scented flower, how can I not throw arms wide and breathe in the clean air, heart bursting with happiness. After all the hard work of pruning, I can't help saying, 'Thank you darling'. The roses which ramble through the lilac racemes of wisteria (the clotted cream 'Lamarque' and 'Yellow Charles Austin') are doing what I imagined, when I planned and planted, all those years ago. As no-one is watching, I lie on the grass beneath and croon with joy.

In the vegie garden, things are a little different. Demanding prima donnas, vegetables seem to say, 'You expect me to perform for your visitors, you need me to look good, so pamper me'.

At Christmas, great swathes of *Lilium* 'Devon Dawn' in the long border are flamboyant, yet stately. Their elegant spires give hope to a planting that shows my mistakes and so I say to them, wryly, 'Thank goodness for you'.

Around the house, in January, the easiest of the lilies, the highly perfumed Christmas lily (*Lilium longiflorum*) return year after year, at the same time as the *Jasminum azoricum* is covered in starry, white scented flowers. The white wisteria, *Wisteria floribunda* 'Alba', spot-flowers and underneath, *Hosta fortunei* 'Aureomarginata' creates a peaceful tapestry.

How can you not tell them all just how much you love them?

Opposite: A collection of shrubs and perennials lead to a pavilion.

Above: Spring at Rowandale.

Left: A backdrop of local gums *E. robertsonii* frames the garden.

Below: Dry stone walls support beds of bulbs and groundcovers.

General index

Aberfoyle, 10–11
Adelaide, 54–55, 82–83, 120–121, 138–139, 152–153, 168
Adelaide's Botanic Gardens, 168
Al Ru Farm, 40, 104
Albers, Hans and Gil, 57
Alton, 116–117
Angas, Alastair and Janet, 179
Anlaby station, 57
Arnold, Joan, 105, 108–109, 110
Australian National Botanic Garden, 111
Avon Valley Historical Rose Garden, 174

Baker, Robyn and Bill, 113
Barossa Valley, 40
Barrabool Hills Maze and Gardens, 81
Barrett, Don, 138–139
Bebeah, 70–71
Bellrive, 135
Belmont, 74–75
Benara Homestead, 105
Bennett, John, 122–123
Berger, Virginia, 76–77
Bickerton, Professor Ian, 186–187
Black Springs Bakery 38–39, 105, 165
Blackdown, 26–27
Blazey, Clive and Penny, 160–161
Black Mountain, 111
Blue Mountains, 26–27
Bouman, Wilmar, 124–125, 165
Bowley, Pat and Judy, 46–47
Boxford, 31
Brockhoff, Fiona, 62
Brooke, Florence, 61
Brookland Valley Vineyard, 130
Buderim, 50–51
Burke, Don, 108, 128–129
Burke, Jane, 62
Busker's End, 105, 108–109
Bussell, family 22–23
Byrne, Barry, 70–71

Cambadello, 114
Cameron, Robyn, 28–29
Camillo, Julie, 36
Campbell, Allan, 80
Campbell, Geoff and Roma, 146–147
Campbell-Wemys, Valerie, 58–59
Canberra, 31, 56, 76–77, 111
Carn, Shirley, 45
Cassidy, Peg and Harry, 108
Cedars, The, 80
Central Coast, NSW, 48–49, 94–95, 108
Cherry, Bob, 94–95
Clare Ranges, 176–177, 179
Cloudehill, 58–59, 104
Coal Seam Gully, 143
Collee, Marcelle, 30
Collins, Harvey, 138–139
Collyer, Mary, 148–149
Combadello, 114
Cooinda, 88–89
Cooke, Graham and Lesley, 72–73
Coonawarra District, 21
Corinda, 124–125
Cowell, Rob, 38–39, 105, 165
Crawford, Elizabeth, 86–87
Cullen, Shelley, 162, 170–171
Cullen, Shirley, 64–65
Cullen Winery, 171
Culpepper's, 36, 185

Daly, Rhonda and Bill, 66
Dalziell, Lindy and Hamish, 50–51
Dandenong Ranges, 45, 58–59, 104
Delmont, 166–167
Dexter, Eva, 162
Ditchfield, 115
Doshong La, 136–137
Downer, Nicky, 165
Dudley, John and Corrie, 85
Duncan, Jean, 41
Duncan, Walter, 176–177
Dunedin, 182
Dunkeld, 24
Duxfield, Geoff, 115

Elizabeth Town Nursery, 85
Ellensbrook, 22
Eshuys, Marj and Ed, 116–117
Eudlo Cycad Gardens, 131

Fairhill, 142
Falkiner, Rose and David, 34–35
Faulkner, Simon, 174
Fauser, Otto, 136–137
Fawkner family, 74–75
Forge, Sue and Warwick, 156
Francis, Jeremy, 58–59, 104
Freudenstein, Sandy, 13
Friesia, 156

Gall, Christine, 134
Geelong, 81
Geelong's Botanic Gardens, 163
Gerchow, Lindsay, 135
Glebe, The, 134
Gledswood, 42–43
Glen, The, 14–15
Glenn, David, 32–33
Glenrock, 158–159
Goodman, Dale, 173
Graham, Betty, 15
Grampians, 24, 90–91, 146–147
Guilfoyle, William Robert, 20

Hansen, Barbara, 142
Harvey, Lois, 48–49
Havelberg, Dean, 104, 154–155
Hays, Tim, 122–123
Hawkins, Elizabeth and Thomas, 26–27
Heirbloem, Peter, 131
Henderson, Stewart, 61, 105
Heronswood, 160–161
Heysen, Sir Hans and Nora, 80
Hill River Station, 179
Hillview, 104
Hollywood Reserve, 96–97, 183
Honeysuckle Gardens, 30
Hopmeier, Paul, 92–93
Hurditch, Chris, 115

Invergowrie, 78–79
Irving, Ruth, 40
Isaacs, Sam, 22

Jolly Farmer, 18–19
Joyce, Ray, 184–185
Juniper, Bec, 162

Kibbenjelok, 126–127
King, Jan, 92–93
Klok, Gay and Kees, 126–127

Lambley Nursery and Garden, 32–33
Langleigh, 28–29
Lansell, Jenny and Cyril, 140–141
Lawson, Andrew, 26–27
Learmont, Dr. Jenny, 186–187
Leitch, Ruth, 114
Lewis, Bob and Betty, 120–121
Lightbody, Barbara, 10–11
Lismore, 68
Lockwood, Leslie, 111
Lomas, Lloyd and Tricia, 150
Longford Hall, 34–35
Lunch on the Pond, 54–55

Macarthur District, 42–43
McWilliams, Michael, 18–19
Macedon Ranges, 116–117
Magyar, Gabriel, 171
Maiden, Joseph Henry, 51
Malmsbury, 186–187
Margaret River, 64–65, 130, 162, 170–171
Matcham Valley Plant Place, 108
Maune, Di, 88–89
Maxwell, Alan, 12
Melbourne, 20, 156
Melbourne's Royal Botanic Gardens, 20
Milgadara, 66–67
Mistydowns, 90
Mitchell, James, 78
Moat's Corner, 41
Moffatt, Doug, 78–79
Molloy, Georgiana, 22
Moore, Gabrielle and Stephen, 68
Moors, Dr. Phillip, 20
Mornington Peninsula, 41, 62–63, 140–141, 160–161
Morrison, Judy, 90–91
Mount Gambier, 10–11, 105
Mount George, 120–121
Mount Lofty Botanical Garden, 83
Mount Wilson, 70–71

New Norcia, 84
Neale, Helen and Kenneth, 26–27
Northern NSW, 86–89, 114, 122–123
Northern Tablelands, NSW, 26–27, 78–79, 158–159
Nottle, Trevor, 82, 152–153, 164–165

Organic Garden, The, 162
Otway Ranges, 16–17

Pannell, Bill and Sandra, 151
Paradise Plants, 94–95
Parks, Polly and Peter, 31
Parliament House, 56
Paton, Dr. William, 74–75
Persse, Michael Collins, 30
Perth, 84, 96–97, 151, 175, 183
Peterkin, Dr. Mike, 171
Piero Winery, 170–171
Price, Russell, 13
Price of Peace, The, 13

Queensland, 14–15, 134
Quigley, Judith, 54–55

Racecourse Inn, 112–113
Reagan, Jennifer, 122–123
Redlands, 172–173

Retter, Michael, 56
Rigney, Sally and Allen, 166–167
Roberts, Wendy, 175
Robinson, Carolyn and Peter, 158–159
Romantic Cottage Gardens, 72–73
Rowandale, 188–189
Rushbrooke, Elaine, 184–185
Russell, Lynne, 16
Russelldown Garden and Rare Poultry, 16–17
Ryan, Matthew, 124–125
Rymill, Andrew and Peter, 21
Rymill Winery, 21

Scamps, Michele, 173
Scented Rose, The, 184–185
Scott, Annabel, 182
Seccull, Richard, 81
Shady Tree, 30
Shann, Charles and Rowan, 14–15
Shaw, Peggy, 157
Sherwood, 146–147
Smith, Jenny, 81
South Australia, 80, 105, 165, 176–177, 179
South Western NSW, 13
Southern Highlands, 46–47, 104, 115, 154–155, 172–173, 186–187
Stanbridge, Rt. Hon. William Edward, 60
Stirling, 54–55
Stowe, Barry, 36
Summers, John, 23
Sunshine Coast, 12, 36–37, 50–51, 131, 135, 142, 148–149
Sydney, 30, 98–99, 150, 180–181
Sykes, Gordon and Ann, 180–181

Tanner, Howard, 98–99
Tasmania, 18, 74–75, 85, 112–113, 124–127, 165, 166–167, 182, 184–185
Telford, Ian, 78–79
Testoni, Theresa, 42–43
Tinker, Allan and Lorraine, 143

Valder, Dr. Peter, 130
Victoria, 32–33, 38–39, 60–61, 72–73, 105, 108, 157, 163, 165, 169, 178
View's End, 178

Waddington, Jan, 169
Walnut Hill, 152–153
Watervale, 176–177
Welsh, Claire, 96–97, 132–133
Western Australia, 22, 132–133, 143
Western Flora Caravan Park, 143
Whitsunday Islands, 69
Wildes Meadow, 46–47
Willawong, 140–141
Wombat Park, 60–61, 105
Wright, Kaye and Lindsay, 178

Yandina's Ginger Factory, 12
Yves, Danny, 135

Index of plants